The Austin Handbook

Caroline Campbell Robertson

Published by
Hill Country Welcome Service
Austin, Texas
512/219-9476

To
Patricia Campbell Page
Mary Jane Campbell Kelly

Contents

Austin Quick-Tour

Enjoy the scenery as you ride through the hill country on the HILL COUNTRY FLYER, an excursion train powered by a restored steam engine 477-8468
Page 45

Learn about wildflowers and native plants at the NATIONAL WILDFLOWER RESEARCH CENTER 282-4100
Page 62

See if you can locate 17 of the original MOONLIGHT TOWERS that still illuminate Austin with artificial moonlight.
Page 76

Texas history will come to life as you walk through the TEXAS STATE CEMETERY. You will see the final resting place of such heroes as Stephen F. Austin, John Connally and Barbara Jordan 463-0605
Page 68

Ride a train, paddle a canoe, fly a kite, swim in the springs at Austin's own ZILKER PARK 867-3080
Page 64

Take a tour of the STATE CAPITOL and see for yourself why Texans believe their capitol is the largest 475-3070
Page 46

Read the Texas Declaration of Independence, visit the LORENZO DE ZAVALA STATE LIBRARY .. 463-5460
Page 48

Grab a bite to eat and see the handiwork of local artists at the OLD BAKERY AND EMPORIUM 477-5961
Page 50

Take note of the HISTORIC COMMERCIAL BUILDINGS as you drive down Congress Avenue and Historic Sixth Street.
Pages 50-58

From dinosaurs to modern art can be explored at one of the many excellent MUSEUMS.
Page 77

CAPITOL COMPLEX VISITOR'S CENTER is located in the General Land Office Building, the oldest government office building in Texas. 305-4800
Page 48

See the peacocks at MAYFIELD PARK 499-6700
Page 62

Enjoy the view of the UT CAMPUS from the observation deck of the UT Tower.
Page 71

Take the tour of the GOVERNOR'S MANSION, the executive residence of Texas since 1856 463-5518
Page 49

Visit TREATY OAK where legend has it Stephen F. Austin signed a treaty with the Indians.
Page 62

Learn who ELIZABET NEY was and see her unique home and studio 458-2255
Pages 74 and 85

Campout at on of the areas STATE PARKS
Page 133

Enjoy the spectacular sight of 1.5 million BATS emerging from under the Congress Avenue Bridge at sunset 327-9721
Page 63

There are, count them, 99 steps leading to the top of MOUNT BONNELL, the highest point in the city limits.
Page 62

Speaking of city limits, get yourself a ticket to the live taping of AUSTIN CITY LIMITS, but you have to be quick, tickets are limited and it's first come, first served.
Page 98

Cheer for the ICE BATS 927-7825
Page 120

Spend the day at one of the HIGHLAND LAKE PARKS.
Page 134

From Cowchips

to Microchips

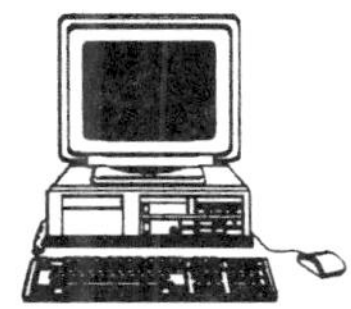

Austin Headlines

1836 On April 21, at the Battle of San Jacinto, Texas won its independence from Mexico and a new nation, the Republic of Texas became a reality.

1836 Interim president, David G. Burnet called for the first election of a President of the Republic. In September Sam Houston won this election, also the Constitution was ratified and a referendum in favor of annexation was passed.

1838 Mirabeau Lamar succeeded Sam Houston as President. The Republic needed a permanent location for the capital. Lamar recommended an area of rolling hills on the Colorado River near the little settlement of Waterloo. In 1837 he had camped there while on a hunting trip with his friend, Jacob Harrell, who had a homestead on Shoal Creek.

1839 A commission was formed to choose a location for the Capital of the Republic. They chose the little settlement of Waterloo and changed the name to Austin, in honor of Stephen F. Austin, the Father of Texas.

1839 Edwin Waller was assigned the job of designing and supervising the construction of the town. He designated areas for parks, and chose the hill overlooking the Colorado River as the future site for Capitol Square, where he envisioned a building as grand as this new country.

1839 The first public land sale was held August 1, 1839. The auction brought in $182,000 for 306 lots. The prices ranged from $120 to $2,800 per lot.

1839 The first capitol in Austin was a log cabin, built on the site where Austin's City Hall is today. The government furniture and the Archives of the Republic had to be moved from Houston in ox carts. In October, when President Lamar arrived, Congress convened in Austin for the first time.

1840 According to the 1840 census, Austin had a population of 806, representing every nation. There were 100 houses, six inns, nine grocers, one billiard hall, two silversmiths, two printing offices, two tailors and six gambling houses.

1840 Edwin Waller was unanimously elected the first mayor of Austin with 187 votes.

1841 Sam Houston succeeded Lamar as President of the Republic. Not surprisingly, Houston never wanted Austin to be the capital. In 1842, when Mexico attacked San Antonio, Houston used safety as an excuse to move the capital back to Houston.

1842 ARCHIVES WAR: Austinites suspected that Sam's ultimate motive for moving the capital was his desire to have Houston as the capital of Texas. When he sent a company of rangers to load the government documents in wagons, Angelina Eberly, the owner of a boarding house, fired a cannon to alert Austinites. Houston's men were defeated and the archives were safely hidden in Eberly's boarding house. A vigilance committee was formed to guard the archives and to search all departing wagons.

1844 Anson Jones was elected President of the Republic and moved the capital back to Austin.

1845 Texas was admitted to the Union as the 28th state. Jones turned over control of the government to the first elected Governor, J. Pickney Henderson. The city of Austin was named the state capital through the year 1850.

1848 The annexation of Texas resulted in the Mexican American War. This time Texans had the United States Army on their side. Mexico finally relinquished all claims to Texas.

1850 In a statewide election, the city of Austin was designated capital of Texas for the next 20 years.

1853 The legislature convened for the first time in the new capitol building, built on Capitol Square.

1856 Governor Pease hosted a public reception honoring the completion of the Governor's Mansion.

1861 Texas seceded from the Union. The citizens of Austin and Travis County voted against the resolution, 704 to 450 votes. From the steps of the Governor's Mansion, Sam Houston gave a passionate speech against secession. It was to no avail and Houston was deposed as Governor and replaced by Lt. Governor Edward Clark.

1865 On June 19, 1865 Union General, Gordon Granger proclaimed that all slaves were free. This day has been celebrated by Texans as Emancipation Day, popularly called Juneteenth.

1865 Andrew Jackson Hamilton was appointed interim Governor of Texas. In October, General George Armstrong Custer and his Union Calvary arrived in Austin to support Reconstruction.

1869 The first pontoon bridge to span the Colorado River at Austin opened.

1871 The railroad arrived in Austin.

1872 Austin was once and for all declared the capital in a state wide election.

1876 The first wooden bridge to span the Colorado River at Austin took 18 months to complete. Soon after it was open a rancher attempting to take his herd of cattle over the bridge caused the bridge to collapse and most of the cattle drowned.

1876 Austin's first public school opened with less than 1000 students. Today this building is used by the Austin ISD as Pease Elementary School.

1881 The stone and wood capitol, built in 1853, was destroyed by fire.

1883 A temporary capitol was completed on the southwest corner of 11th Street and Congress Avenue. The newly established University of Texas held its first classes here in September with 221 students and eight professors.

1884 Old Main, the first building to be completed on the University of Texas campus opened for classes.

1885 St. Edward's College was established.

1886 The Driskill Hotel was completed.

1888 The new state Capitol was completed, and Edwin Waller's vision of a capitol worthy of Texas was realized.

1890 Austinites approved a bond to finance a dam across the Colorado River. When the dam was constructed, it created Lake McDonald, known today as Lake Austin.

1891 Monroe Shipe, developer of Hyde Park, connected this neighborhood in far north Austin with the city using his own electrical streetcar system.

1895 Austin was bathed in artificial moonlight when the 31 towers were illuminated for the first time. The electricity was generated by the new dam.

1900 Heavy rains and a build up of silt caused the collapse of the dam. Huge pieces of granite 8 feet wide and 25 feet thick were sent tumbling down the Colorado River. Within 20 minutes massive flooding occurred when the river became 60 feet deep and a mile wide. It wasn't until the 1930's that the Tom Miller Dam was built. Today chunks of granite from the original dam can be seen beneath the Tom Miller Dam.

1904 The Pasteur Institute located on the grounds of the State Hospital discovered the rabies vaccine.

1905 Bricks were used to pave several blocks of Congress Avenue, making it the first paved street in Austin.

1908 The Austin Women Suffrage Association was formed to gain recognition that women were citizens and should not be denied the right to vote along with "idiots, imbeciles, aliens and the insane".

1909 A park system was established with the opening of Wooldridge Park.

1918 Austin's first supermarket, Piggly Wiggly opened.

1918 The city of Austin acquired Barton Springs from Andrew Zilker with the stipulation that the city would pay $100,000 to the Austin Public School System.

1923 The grand opening of the women's restroom on Congress Avenue created a haven for women and children while the men attended to business. It was complete with tables and chairs, writing desks, typewriters and telephones, cribs and beds. If they only had Happy Meals ......

1926 Concordia Lutheran College was founded.

1926 Austin's first public library opened on Congress Avenue.

1930 Robert Mueller Airport opened.

1935 The UT Tower was completed.

1937 Lyndon Baines Johnson won his first election as a U. S. Representative.

1938 The LCRA began the construction of seven dams which gave the Austin area a 163 mile water wonderland called the Highland Lakes.

1946 The city of Austin purchased the right-of-way for IH-35.

1948 Emma Long was the first woman to serve on the Austin City Council.

1952 KTBC went on the air on Thanksgiving Day with Austin's first television show, the UT vs. Texas A&M football game.

1955 The city of Austin acquired the right of way for MoPac Expressway.

1962 The first Aqua Festival was held on Town Lake.

1966 Barbara Jordan was elected to the Texas Senate, making her the first African American to be elected to the state senate since Reconstruction

1967 IBM started production in Austin.

1970 The Armadillo World Headquarters opened and would eventually change Austin into the Live Music Capital of the World.

1973 A Texas tradition was started with Willie Nelson's first Fourth of July picnic.

1973 With the opening of its manufacturing plant, Motorola will become the largest private employer in the city by the 1980's.

1974 Willie Nelson taped the pilot performance for Austin City Limits. This innovative show, spotlighting the music scene in Austin, became a nationwide public television program in 1976.

1982 The Percy V. Pennybacker Bridge, spanning Lake Austin at Loop 360 was dedicated.

1984 Michael Dell started Dell Computers and will become the largest Austin based company.

1985 *SouthXSouthwest* held its premier music and media conference.

1988 Sematech moved to Austin. This reinforced the city's importance in the world of microelectronics.

1992 The Austin Convention Center opened.

1993 Bergstrom Air Force Base closed and the city took over control for the new Austin Bergstrom International Airport.

1995 After Six years and $187 million dollars the magnificent restoration and expansion of the capitol was completed.

1996 Samsung chose Austin to build microchips.

1998 UT running back Ricky Williams broke the 20 year NCAA record for rushing yards previously held by Tony Dorsett.

1999 The Austin-Bergstrom International Airport opened for passenger flights.

1999 After being closed for over 30 years, the observation deck on the University of Texas Tower was opened to the public.

Info ...

Stuff you need to know

EMERGENCY ... 911

Police ... Fire ... Ambulance ... Sheriff

AREA HOSPITALS

Brackenridge Hospital **324-7000**
601 East 15th Street, Austin

Childrens Hospital **324-8000**
601 East 15th Street, Austin

Georgetown Hospital **943-3000**
2000 Scenic Drive, Georgetown

Heart Hospital of Austin **407-7000**
911 West 38th Street, Austin

North Austin Medical Center **901-1000**
12221 North Mopac, Austin

Round Rock Hospital **341-1000**
2400 Round Rock Avenue, Round Rock

Seton Highland Lakes .... **(512)756-6000**
U.S. 281 South, Burnet

Seton Medical Center **323-1000**
1201 West 38th Street, Austin

Seton Northwest Hospital **795-1000**
11113 Research Blvd., Austin

St. David's Medical Center **476-7111**
919 East 32nd Street, Austin

St. David's South Hospital **447-2211**
901 West Ben White Blvd., Austin

Poison Control .800/764-7661
800/POISON1

24-Hour Pharmacies

Eckerd 835-6751
11300 North Lamar

HEB No.3 459-8308
Hancock Shopping Center

Walgreens
Capital Plaza, IH-35- Cameron Road 452-9451
Stassney at South 1st Street 441-4747

Hospice

Hospice Austin 342-4700
Lone Star Hospice 467-7423

Non-Emergency

For information or non-emergencies

Police Departments

Austin 480-5000
Cedar Park 258-2800
Georgetown 930-3510
Lakeway 261-6090
Lago Vista 267-7141
Leander 259-0613
Pflugerville 251-4004
Round Rock 218-5500
West Lake Hills 327-1195

Travis County Sheriff 473-9285
Williamson County Sheriff 930-3200

Road Conditions

Texas Road Condition Hotline
800/452-9292
Austin streets closed due to storms
440-8444
Austin streets closed due to construction
499-7024

Utilities

Electricity

City of Austin 476-7721
Emergency 322-9100
Pederanales 219-2602
Emergency 331-8883
TU Electric 800/242-9113
Emergency 800/233-2133

Natural Gas

Lone Star Gas 800/460-3030
Emergency 800/817-8090
Southern Union Gas 800-706-2443
Emergency 800-959-5325

Water

City of Austin 476-7721
Emergency 912-6000
City of Cedar Park 258-6651
Emergency 258-5115
City of Lago Vista 267-1155
Emergency 267-7141

Leander 259-1142
    Emergency 259-0613
Round Rock 218-5555
    Emergency 218-5580

Telephone

Southwestern Bell 800/464-7928
    Emergency 800/246-8464

Cable

Time Warner Communications 485-5555
Serves Austin, Lago Vista, West Lake Hills

Heartland Wireless 800-876-6299
Austin and surrounding areas

CableVision of Lake Travis 263-9194
Serves Lakeway and Lake Travis

CableVision 930-3085
Serves Georgetown, Leander, Pflugerville

Child Abuse Hotline .. **800/252-5400**
To report cases of child abuse

Crime Stoppers **472-8477**
To report information about a crime

Drug Hotline **454-3784**
To report drug activity

Elderly and Disabled Abuse **800/252-5400**
To report cases of abuse of the elderly or disabled

Gang Hotline **480-5261**
To report gang activity

Graffiti Hotline **473-4125**
For assistance in having graffiti removed

Mental Heath **472-HELP**
For psychiatric emergencies of children and adults; alcohol and drug abuse problems

Missing Children **800/843-5678**
To report a missing child

Neighborhood Watch **926-9932**
For information about a program in your neighborhood

SAFEPLACE
Domestic violence and Sexual Assault Survival Center
Domestic Violence Crisis Hotline **928-9070**
Sexual Assault Crisis Hotline **440-7273**
Resource Center **385-5181**

SAFEPLACE accepts donations of clothing, household items and toys.
For pick-up of your donations call **451-4108**

Weather

Time and Temp 973-3555

5-Day Forecast Recordings

KTBC 476-7744
KVUE 451-2424

Average Temperatures: 42-62 degrees in winter
75-95 degrees in summer
Average Rainfall: 32 inches

Weather Terms & Precautions

Watch: Conditions exist for the **POSSIBILITY** of a severe thunderstorm, tornado or flash flood.

Warning: A tornado, severe thunderstorm or flash flooding **HAS BEEN SEEN OR DETECTED** by radar.

Flash Flooding: When conditions create rapidly rising water stay away from creeks and low water crossings; do not drive through water covering the road; heed all warnings and street barricades. Do not let children play around creeks or drainage ditches.

Thunderstorms: Stay indoors away from windows. If outdoors do not stand under trees, seek shelter in a low lying area. Do not use the telephone.

Tornadoes: Stay indoors away from windows. If you are in a vehicle or mobile home seek shelter in a ditch or low lying area.

Ozone Action Days

Ground-level ozone, a major component of smog, forms when pollutants react in sunlight. Ozone formation is greatest on sunny, hot, windless days from April through October.

Things you can do on an Ozone Action Day

- Limit your driving and delay running errands
- Ride the bus -- it is free on Ozone Action Days
- Share a ride to work or school
- Walk or ride a bicycle to work or school
- Keep your vehicle, lawn mower and boat engine properly tuned
- Avoid using lighter fluid when firing-up the barbecue grill
- Postpone refueling until after 5 pm and don't top-off the tank
- Avoid drive-thru lanes
- Postpone using gas powered equipment until after 5 pm

Daylight Savings starts the first Sunday in April at 2am.

Standard Time starts the last Sunday in October at 2am.

Pets & Wild Animals

What to do if armadillos set up their new headquarters in your yard!

Animal Control

Austin 472-7387
Cedar Park 258-3149
Georgetown 930-3592
Leander 259-0613
Pflugerville 251-4004
Round Rock 255-7387

Pet Adoption

Town Lake Animal Shelter 472-7387
1156 West Cesar Chavez Street
Humane Society of Austin 837-7985
124 West Anderson Lane
Williamson County 388-4816
2121 North Mays, Round Rock

Wildlife Rescue

The return of animals to their natural habitat
Austin 472-9453

Animal Vaccinations: In Travis and Williamson counties cats and dogs must be vaccinated against rabies.

Leash Law: In Austin dogs cannot run loose; in Williamson County this goes for cats too. Travis County does not require leashes.

Area Curfews

Austin

School Hours: Monday-Friday 9am-2:30pm
Unsupervised children under the age of 17 are not allowed in public places when school is in session.

Exceptions: People under the age of 17 with a high school diploma; school holidays or excused absences, such as off campus lunch; home-schooled students are not subject to the school hours curfew.

Evening Hours: Sunday-Thursday 11:30pm-6am; Friday-Saturday 12:30am-6am

Unsupervised children under the age of 17 are not allowed on streets or in public places, with the exception of the sidewalk in front of their own home or the home of a neighbor.

Downtown Entertainment District: 10pm-6am
Unsupervised children under the age of 17 are not allowed in the downtown entertainment district.

Dove Springs: Sunday-Thursday 11pm-6am; Friday-Saturday 12am-6am

Children under the age of 17 are not allowed on city streets, alleys, sidewalks, parks, or any place open to the public unless accompanied by their parents or guardians or are on an errand for their parents, or are participating in a religious or job activity.

Cedar Park

School Hours: Monday-Friday 9am-2:30pm

Unsupervised children under the age of 17 are not allowed in public places when school is in session.

Exceptions: Work or religious related activities.

Evening Hours: Monday-Thursday 11pm-6am; Friday -Saturday 1am-6am

Unsupervised children under the age of 17 are not allowed in public places.

Round Rock

Evening Hours: Monday-Friday 12:01am-6am; Saturday-Sunday 1am-6am

Unsupervised children under age 17 are not allowed on streets or in public places.

Driving in Texas

Safety Belts & Child Seats:

All front seat occupants must wear auto safety belts. Children between the ages of two and four must be secured in either a safety belt or a child safety seat. Children age two and younger must be secured in a child safety seat.

Pickup Trucks:

If carrying passengers under the age of 12 in the truck bed, do not exceed a speed of 35 m.p.h.

Texas law prohibits the consumption of alcoholic beverages by the driver of any vehicle.

If you are involved in an accident:

You do not have to call the police to the scene of an accident unless there is an injury or a wrecker is needed.

If the situation does not warrant a call to the police, get the other driver's insurance information, driver's license number and vehicle license plate number.

If there is an injury or either vehicle has over $500 in damage, an accident report must be filed within 10 days.

Call the police to the scene whenever you are in doubt or are suspicious about the credibility of the other driver's information.

Proof of Liability Insurance:

You cannot legally operate a motor vehicle in Texas without liability insurance coverage. Proof of liability insurance must be presented for a vehicle safety inspection, applying for or renewing your vehicle registration, applying for or renewing your driver's license or requested by a police officer.

Vehicle Safety Inspection

A yearly inspection is required for every car, truck, motorcycle, moped, trailer, semitrailer, pole trailer, or travel trailer registered in Texas and operated on a public roadway.

A valid vehicle inspection sticker must be displayed on the lower left corner of the winshield.

Cost: $10.50
What to bring:
Proof of insurance

Vehicle inspections are conducted at official state appointed vehicle inspection stations.

Vehicle Registration

New residents have 30 days to register their vehicles in the **county** where they reside. You are exempt if you are a full time student paying out of state tuition. You can renew your vehicle registration by mail or at most local grocery stores.

Travis County Tax Office **473-9473**
1010 Lavaca Street, Austin, Texas 78701

Williamson County Tax Offices

Georgetown:
8th & Main Street
930-4305

Round Rock:
211 Commerce Street
244-3278

What to Bring:
Green certificate from inspection station,
Car title or registration receipt from previous state,
Proof of liability insurance.

Driver's License

New Texas residents must obtain a driver's license within 30 days. Full time students, paying out of state tuition, may use the driver's license of their home state. If you move within the state you have 30 days to make a change of address.

Austin:
6121 North Lamar Blvd. **424-2076**
13730 Research Blvd. **335-8131**
4719 South Congress Avenue **444-5241**
Georgetown:
515 Pine Street **863-5816**

Eligibility:
16 years of age and completion of driver's education.
18 years of age if you do not take driver's education.

Test:
Driving skills test, written test and vision exams are required. The driving skills test is waived with proof of lab phase of driver's education. If an applicant has a valid out of state license, the driving skills test and written test will be waived with proof ofinsurance and Texas registration.

What to bring:

When making initial application:

1. Your birth certificate or other qualified evidence which documents the date of your birth.

2. Social security number

3. Proof of auto insurance and vehicle registration.

To renew or change your address you must present proof of auto insurance.

Cost:	$20.00	Five year license
	$24.00	Six year license
	$15.00	Motorcycle
	$60.00	Commercial
	$10.00	Duplicate
	$10.00	Change of address

Birth & Death Certificates

State Health Department **469-2031**
1100 West 49th Street
P.O. Box 10240
Austin, Texas 78711-2040

Hours: Monday-Friday 8am-5pm

Searching Fees: $11.00 Birth Certificate
$ 9.00 Death Certificate

Certified copies of birth and death certificates can be obtained in person or by mail. If applying by mail, send the searching fee and the following information:

Name, date and place of birth or death of the person on the certificate requested.

Full name of the individual's father and mother, including mother's maiden name.

Your purpose for obtaining the certificate.

Your relationship to the person named on the certificate.

Your daytime phone number.

Your handwritten signature and return address.

A photocopy of your picture I.D.

If you are not an immediate family member or a legal representative, you must also include a notarized statement from the individual named on the certificate or an immediate family member.

Voter Registration

Eligibility: You must be a U.S. Citizen, 18 years of age, a resident of the county in which you intend to vote and registered to vote at least 30 days prior to any election.

How to register: Applications may be made in person, or mailed to your county registrar of voters. Applications are available at DPS Offices, Federal Offices, U.S. Post Offices, public libraries and most local grocery stores. Applications may also be ordered by phone from your county registrar. Once you are registered you will receive a new voter's certificate by mail every two years.

Travis County Registrar **473-9473**
1010 Lavaca Street
Austin, Texas 78701

Williamson County Registrar **930-4300**
8th & Main Street
Georgetown, Texas 78626

Change of Address: If you move within the county, you must update your address by calling the county tax office. If your county of residence changes, you must reregister.

Early voting: All qualified voters may vote early by personal appearance. No reason is needed. Qualified voters may vote early by mail if: you will be absent from your county on election day and during the period to vote early in person; you are disabled; you are 65 years of age or older on election day; you are confined to jail.

Jury Duty: Jury summons are randomly selected from driver's license and voter registration lists.

Passport

Applications can be made at the Post Office.
Applicants must be present.

The following information must be presented:

- Proof of citizenship (certified birth certificate)
- Proof of identity (valid driver's license)
- 2 passport photographs.

There is a $65.00 registration fee.
A passport takes 4 to 6 weeks to process.

Marriage License

Travis County Courthouse....... 473-9188
West 11th at Guadalupe, Room 222
Austin, Texas 78701

Williamson County Courthouse
930-4304
8th & Main Street, Georgetown, Texas 78626

Couple must be present to apply.
There is a $31.00 fee which must be paid in cash.
The license is good for 30 days.
There is a 72 hour waiting period

Present one of the following forms of identification:
Valid driver's license, passport, military I.D., or certified copy of birth certificate.

Texas Lottery

So you want to be a Texas Millionaire?

Austin Claim Center 344-5252
Lottery Commission 344-5000

You must be 18 years old to play.

Winning tickets must be claimed within 180 days after the draw date on your ticket.

A winning ticket is a bearer instrument
DON'T LOSE IT

Taxes in Texas

There is no state income tax in Texas, however we do pay sales tax, and property tax. Your property taxes can be reduced if you file for a homestead exemption. If you are over 65 years old, you qualify for an additional reduction. Apply for your exemptions at your county tax office.

If you need the Feds

Federal Building
300 East 8th Street
Austin, TX 78701

Secret Service **916-5103**
Small Business Administration **916-5288**
Social Security Administration **800/772-1213**
Internal Revenue Service
Automated Refund & Tele-Tax **800/829-4477**
Federal Tax Forms **800/829-3676**
Federal Tax Information **800/829-1040**
Note: No walk in tax help is given at the Service Center
FBI **345-1111**

United States Senators

Phil Gramm **202/224-2934**
Russell Senate Office Building, Room 370
Washington, D.C. 20510
Kay Bailey Hutchison **202/224-5922**
Russell Senate Office Building, Room 284
Washington, D.C. 20510

United States Representatives:

LLoyd Doggett **202/225-4865**
(Travis County)
Cannon House Office Building, Room 126
Washington, D.C. 20515

Lamar Smith **202/225-4236**
(Williamson County)
Rayburn House Office Building, Room 2231
Washington, D.C. 20515

Ron Paul **202/225-2831**
(Travis, Williamson, Hays, Bastrop & Caldwell Counties)
Cannon House Office Building, Room 203
Washington, D.C. 20515

Postal Services

Austin General Mail Facility
8225 Cross Park Drive

Recorded Information and Rates **342-1253**
Zip Code Information **342-1255**
Balcones Station **331-7737**
11900 Jollyville Road
Bluebonnet Station **834-8930**
1822 West Braker Lane
Capitol Station **477-4240**
Chimney Corners Station **345-4240**
7116 Chimney Corners
Downtown Station **494-2200**
510 Guadalupe Street
East Austin Station **472-2644**
1914 East 6th Street

Mockingbird Station **416-1177**
7310 Manchaca Road
North Austin Station **453-7252**
4300 Speedway
Northcross Station **454-4581**
7700 Northcross Drive
Northeast Station **451-7556**
900 Blackson
Oak Hill Station **892-5501**
6104 Old Fredericksburg Road
South Austin Station **444-6728**
1800 South 5th Street
Southeast Station **444-3118**
4516 Burleson Road
Town North PO Box Unit **835-5355**
8557 Research Blvd.
UT Station **471-8867**
West Mall
Cedar Park **258-1133**
305 South Bell
Georgetown **863-2325**
2300 Scenic Drive
Lago Vista **267-3187**
5803 Thunderbird
Leander **259-1111**
801 Us Hwy 183 South
Pflugerville **251-4133**
103 South Railroad Avenue
Round Rock **255-3516**
797 Sam Bass Road
2250 Double Creek Drive
Westlake Station **328-5690**
3217 Bee Caves Road

State Government

Governor George W. Bush 463-2000
Lt. Governor Rick Perry 463-0001
Comptroller Carol Rylander 463-4000

City of Austin

124 West 8th Street

Mayor's Office 499-2250
City Council Agenda Information 499-2210
City of Austin Switchboard 499-2000
Information "City Connection" 499-2489
Capital Metro 474-1200
Environmental Hotline 499-2550
Keep Austin Beautiful 499-3577
Parks & Recreation 499-6700

City Hall

Cedar Park 258-4121
Mayor's Office 331-6263
600 North Bell Blvd.
Georgetown 930-3723
Mayor's Office 930-3651
609 Main Street
Lago Vista 267-1155
5803 Thunderbird
Lakeway 261-6090
104 Cross Creek

Leander 259-1178
200 Willis Street
Pflugerville 251-3076
100 East Main Street
Round Rock 218-5400
221 East Main Street
West Lake Hills 327-3628
911 Westlake Drive

Chamber of Commerce

Greater Austin Chamber 478-9383
111 Congress Avenue
Capital City Chamber 459-1181
5407 North IH35
Hispanic Chamber 476-7502
823 Congress Avenue
Cedar Park Chamber 258-8007
600 North Bell
Georgetown Chamber 930-3535
100 Stadium Drive
Lago Vista Chamber 267-7952
20264 FM1431, Suite 130
Lake Travis Chamber 263-3188
801 RR 620 South
Leander Chamber 259-1907
304 West South Street
Pflugerville Chamber 251-7799
100 East Main Street
Round Rock 255-5805
212 East Main Avenue

Convention Center, Auditorium & Coliseum

Call for a calendar of events **404-4404**

Convention Center **476-5461**
505 East Cesar Chavez

Palmer Auditorium **472-5111**
400 South 1st Street

City Coliseum **472-5111**
101 Dawson

Austin Visitor's Bureau **478-0098**
201 East 2nd Street

Capitol Complex Visitor's Center **305-4800**
112 East 11th Street

Texas Travel Information......**800/452-9292**

The Texas Department of Transportation has everything you need to Travel Texas! Call for a beautiful, comprehensive book on Texas cities and points of interest, a state calendar of events and a Texas map.

It is FREE for the asking

Traveling to Mexico

Mexican Consulate **478-2866**
200 East 6th Street, Austin, Texas 78701

Hours: Monday-Friday 9am-2pm; closed U.S. Holidays

The purpose of the Consulate is to strengthen the relations between Mexico and the United States.

Climate: Like salsa .... mild, warm, hotter!
Time: Central Standard Time all year
Measures: Metric System
Currency: Peso

All U.S. Citizens must present either a valid passport or a picture I.D. **and** a birth certificate. When traveling into Mexico on business you must have a VISA **and** a valid passport.

Arriving by Plane

A tourist permit is required. This can be obtained at the airport or through your travel agent.

Driving into Mexico

Proof of ownership or a letter stating that you are the person leasing the vehicle. Check with your insurance agent about coverage in Mexico. A $10 vehicle registration fee is required at the border. This fee must be paid by credit card.

Limits on Merchandise Entering the United States

Liquor: 2 liters per person
Cigarettes: 200 cigarettes per person
Cigars: 50 cigars per person

$400 limit if returning by air

Austin Libraries

To obtain a library card you must have a picture ID, proof of address, and a driver's license or social security card. Children applying must be accompanied by an adult with identification.

Children's Programs **499-7599**
Recorded information **499-7302**
John Henry Faulk Central Library **499-7300**
800 Guadalupe
Hours: Monday-Thursday 9am-9pm; Friday-Saturday 9am-6pm Sunday 12pm-6pm

Branches
Hours: Monday-Thursday 10am-9pm; Friday10am-6pm; Weekend hours vary

Carver	1161 Angelina	472-8954
Dove Springs	5405 Pleasant Valley	462-1452
Govalle	4704-A East 1st Street	385-2670
Howson	2500 Exposition	472-3584
Little Walnut Creek	835 W. Rundberg	836-8975
Manchaca	5500 Manchaca	447-6651
North Loop Area	2210 Hancock	454-7208
North Village	2139 W. Anderson Lane	458-2239
Oak Springs	3101 Oak Springs	926-4453
Old Quarry	7051 Village Center	345-4435
Pleasant Hill	211 William Cannon	441-7993
Riverside	2410 E. Riverside Drive	448-0776
Spicewood Springs	8637 Spicewood Springs Rd.	258-9070
Terrazas	1105 East 1st Street	472-7312
Twin Oaks	2301 South Congress Avenue	442-4664
University Hills	4721 Loyola Lane	929-0551
Windsor Village	5825 Berkman	928-0333

Area Libraries

Cedar Park **259-5353**
550 Discovery Blvd.
Hours: Monday-Thursday 9am-8pm;

808 Martin Luther King Street
Hours: Monday-Thursday 10am-8pm;
Friday 10am-6pm; Saturday 10am-3pm

Leander **259-5259**
406 Municipal Drive
Hours: Monday and Wednesday 10am-4pm;
Tuesday and Thursday 3pm-8pm;
Saturday 10am-2pm

Pflugerville **251-9185**
102 South Third Street
Hours: Monday & Wednesday 3pm-6pm
Tuesday & Thursday 10am-7pm;
Saturday 10am-2pm

Round Rock **255-3939**
221 East Main
Hours: Monday-Thursday 10am-9pm;
Friday-Saturday 10am-5pm

Westlake Hills **327-3045**
1309 West Bank Drive
Hours: Monday, Wednesday, Friday 10am-6pm
Tuesday & Thursday 10am-8pm;
Saturday 10am-2pm

Parking and Transportation

Name that Street

Traffic is not the only problem that Austin drivers encounter. Learning all of the names given to the main streets can become the biggest challenge. Depending on the stretch of road you are traveling the name can change and the road can either blend into another or quit and start up on the other side of town.

South 1st	Cesar Chavez
Guadalupe	The Drag
Loop 1	MoPac
FM 1325	Louis Henna; Burnet Road; MoPac
360	The Capital of Texas Highway
RR 620	Marshall Ford Road
US 183	Bell Blvd.; Research Blvd.; Anderson Lane; Ed Bluestein Blvd.
FM 2222	Bull Creek Road; Northland Drive; Koenig Lane; 290
RM 2244	Bee Caves Road
71	Ben White; 290

The downtown streets, running east and west, except for 1st Street, were named for trees.

2nd ..... Live Oak Street
3rd ..... Cypress Street
4th ..... Cedar Street
5th ..... Pine Street
6th ..... Pecan Street
7th ..... Bois de Arc Street
8th ..... Hickory Street
9th ..... Ash Street
10th ..... Mulberry Street
11th ..... Mesquite Street

The downtown streets running north and south, except for Congress Avenue, are named for rivers in Texas: Sabine, Red River, Neches, Trinity, San Jacinto, Brazos, Colorado, Lavaca, Guadalupe, San Antonio, Nueces, Rio Grande. The streets are named in the order the rivers flow through the state.

Austin Downtown Rangers

Rangers provide assistance to residents, visitors and employees, in Downtown Austin and report criminal activity to the Austin Police Department. Patrolling on bike or on foot they carry two-way communication equipment, giving them instant access to Police dispatchers. They are not police; they don't carry weapons or make arrests. If you are downtown and need information or help just ask a Ranger!

Parking Guide

Downtown

Parking Meters
The parking meters on Congress Avenue and the side streets vary in times and fees.

Meter feeding is a violation. You cannot park in a space longer than the maximum time limit.

Free Time: Monday-Friday, 5pm-8:30am
Saturday, Sunday, New Years Day, Fourth of July, Labor Day, Thanksgiving Day, and Christmas Day

Handicap Parking: Vehicles with a handicap permit can park free at all times.

State Parking Lots
Most parking spaces that are reserved for state employees are available at no charge after 5:30pm Monday-Friday and all day Saturday and Sunday.

Paid Lots and Parking Garages
Commercial parking lots and garages that provide public parking display a sign with a blue "P" on a blue triangle. The rates and times vary.

The University of Texas

Parking and Traffic **471-4761**
UT Permit Parking Spaces
Most permit parking spaces become available to the public after 4:00pm Monday-Friday and all day Saturday and Sunday.

Free Parking: Available at the LBJ Library on Red River

Paid Lots: Most paid lots have spaces for the public.

Parking Garages: There are two public garages serving opposite ends of the campus.

North end: 26th & San Jacinto
South end: Whitis (behind Dobie Mall)

Transportation Guide

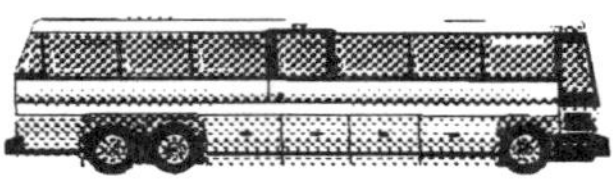

Capital Metro

Customer Service Center
106 East 8th Street **389-7475**
Office Hours: Monday-Friday 7:30am-5:30pm

Rideline **474-1200**
For bus schedule information
Ridefinders **477-7433**
For van and car pool matching
Special Transit Service **478-9647**
Door to door service for the disabled.

Capitol Metro Fares:
One way fixed Route .... **Adult 50 cents**
One way express .... **Adult $1**
Children age 6 and younger ....**Free**

UT Students .... **Free**
(transportation fee is paid at registration
All other students .... **Half-price**
Senior Citizens age 65 and older .... **Free**
(present photo I.D.)
People with disabilities .... **Free**
(present I.D. card issued by Capital Metro)
Ozone Action Days .... **Free**
(to help reduce pollution take the bus on these days)

the'Dillo 474-1200

Call for schedules

Ride 'Dillo trolley routes for **FREE** to downtown, the UT campus, state office complex and restaurants and clubs along Sixth Street.

Congress 'Dillo: Provides circular service to downtown, the state Capitol Complex, and UT from the 'Dillo Park & Ride lot at the City Coliseum.

Lavaca 'Dillo: All day circular service to the Travis County Courthouse and Annex Building, ACC Rio Grande Campus and UT from the 'Dillo Park & Ride lot at the City Coliseum.

Old Pecan Street 'Dillo: Provides crosstown service along 5th, 6th and 7th Street corridors with free parking available at Austin High School Park & Ride.

Taxicabs

Ace Taxi Round Rock	244-1133
American Yellow Checker Cab Co.	452-9999
Roy's Taxi	482-0000
Star Shuttle and Charter	479-8100

Airlines

American Airlines	
Flight Information	800/223-5436
Reservations	800/433-7300
Continental Airlines	
Flight Information	800/784-4444
Reservations	800/231-0856
Delta Airlines	
Flight Information	800/325-1999
Reservations	800/221-1212
Northwest Airlines	
Flight Information	800/441-1818
Reservations	800/225-2525
Southwest Airlines	
Flight Information	800/435-9792
Reservations	800/435-9792
TWA	
Flight Information	800/893-5436
Reservations	800/221-2000
United Airlines	
Flight Information	800/241-6522
Reservations	800/241-6522

Trains

Hill Country Flyer **477-8468**

A steam powered excursion train

Schedules: Operates from March through December

Routes:

Hill Country Flyer .... Cedar Park to Burnet
River City Flyer .... Downtown Austin
San Gabriel Flyer .... Cedar Park to Liberty Hill
Twilight Flyer .... Cedar Park to Liberty Hill

Zilker Eagle Train **478-8167**

Tours through Zilker Park

Hours: Open year round 10am-dusk
Admission: Adult $1.25; Children $1.00

Amtrak **476-5684**
250 North Lamar Blvd.
Reservations **800-872-7245**

Lone Star Attractions

Austin's heritage is unique in that it has been the seat of government for both a nation and a state. In 1839 the settlement of Waterloo was chosen as the Capital of the Republic of Texas and the name was changed to Austin. When Texas became a state in 1845 Austin remained the Capital, but it wasn't until an election in 1872 that the city was officially declared, once and for all, the Capital of Texas.

Many changes have been made to the little wooded settlement along the Colorado River. Fortunately much of the past has been preserved and restored to the original style and finishes.

By seeing where our early neighbors lived and worked we will have a better understanding of who they were and appreciate what life was like for them. Whether you visit a museum, take a walking tour or drive through a historic neighborhood we hope this chapter will help you get to know the men and women who had a vision of a better life and endured many hardships of survival to shape this beautiful city.

The Capitol Complex

State Capitol 475-3070
Congress Avenue and 11th Street
(1888)

Hours: Daily 6:00am-11:00pm
Closed: Thanksgiving Day, December 24, 25, 26 and New Year's Day
Tours: Monday-Friday 8:30am-4:30pm
Saturday and Sunday 9:30am-4:30pm
Tour office is located at the south entrance.
Admission: Free
Legislature: Regular sessions convene in January of odd numbered years and are open to the public. Call for times.

In 1839, when Edwin Waller was laying out the plans for the Capital of the Republic of Texas, he chose this hill top overlooking the Colorado River as the future site of *Capitol Square*. It was not until 1888 that Waller's vision of a Capitol worthy of Texas was to be realized.

The first Capitol was a wood cabin which was built where City Hall stands today (124 West 8th Street). In 1852 a three story stone and wood structure was completed on *Capitol Square*. When this building burned in 1881, a temporary capitol was constructed on the southwest corner of 11th Street and Congress Avenue.

In 1888 the present Capitol was completed. Designed by Architect Elijah Myers, it is modeled after the nation's Capitol in Washington, D.C., and is the largest of the nation's capitols.

The Texas Capitol Restoration Project has restored the capitol to its original grandeur. With great effort and attention to detail the original finishes and architectural design were returned to the building and carried throughout the underground extension. The 620,000 foot extension provides offices for legislatures, committee rooms and underground parking. The unique design of the skylights which run the length of the underground corridor not only add light and openness, but provide a majestic view of the Capitol.

The construction took seven years and cost $3,223,593.

When the capitol was completed it was the seventh largest building in the world.

3,000,000 acres of Texas was sold for 50 cents an acre to fund the project.

The granite was donated by the owners of the granite quarry in Burnet County.

Texans boast it stands seven feet higher than the United States Capitol.

The building crew was local citizens, state prisoners, and stonecutters from Scotland.

Capitol Complex Visitor's Center

General Land Office Building 305-4800
East 11th and Brazos Street
(1857)

Hours: Tuesday-Friday 9am-5pm; Saturday 12pm-5pm
Tours: Self-guided and guided tours are available.
Admission: Free

Visitors are introduced to the history of the capitol complex from the building of the capitol to the extensive preservation project.

The General Land Office was created in 1836. It was responsible for the management, documentation and dispensation of the vast land holdings of the Republic of Texas and later the State of Texas.

State officials fearing for the safety of the records, in case of fire, had this building constructed of limestone. Designed by German architect Conrad Stremme, it is modeled after a German castle. Today it is the oldest surviving government office building in Texas.

From 1887 to 1890 writer, O Henry, worked in the General Land Office as a draftsman. In his short story, "Bexar Scrip No, 2692," written in 1894, he describes the limestone spiral staircase which winds from the bottom floor to the attic.

Lorenzo de Zavala State Library...463-5460

1201 Brazos Street

Hours: Archives: Monday- Friday 8am-5pm
Genealogy: Tuesday-Saturday 8am-5pm

The State Archives include permanent records of Texas Government from the Texas Declaration of Independence, to election returns and personal papers of Texas leaders.

The Genealogy Collection is the primary site for family history research. Census schedules for all states, Texas voter registers, and naturalization records are some of the resources available.

Capitol Building Ruins

Congress Avenue & 11th Street, Southwest corner
(1883)

When the capitol burned in 1881, a temporary statehouse was built on this corner. The building burned in 1899, but its stone foundation remains.

In 1883, the University of Texas also used this building for the first semester of classes, while Old Main was being completed. The enrollment was 221 students and nine professors.

Governor's Mansion 463-5518

1010 Colorado Street
(1856)

Tours: Monday-Friday 10am-11:40am
Admission: Free

This stately mansion has been the executive residence of Texas since 1856, when Elisha M. Pease was Governor. Designed by Abner Cook in the Greek Revival style, it is constructed of hand made bricks; the six pillars are made of pine logs from Bastrop, Texas. Furnishings and memorabilia from former governors are on display on the first floor.

Historic Commercial Buildings

Old Bakery and Emporium 477-5961

1006 Congress Avenue
(1876)
Hours: Monday-Friday 9am-4pm
Saturdays in December, before Christmas, 10am-3pm

Built by Swedish immigrant Charles Lundberg, this building served as a bakery until 1936. Today the bakery has been restored and is operated by the Austin Parks and Recreation Department as a senior citizen's craft project. There is a gift shop with reasonably priced items handcrafted by older artists. The confectionery is an old fashioned coffee shop which offers sandwiches, pastries, coffee and soft drinks.

Jacob Larmour Block

906-920 Congress Avenue
(1876)

Designed by architect Jacob Larmour in the

Italianate Style, these adjoining buildings have housed various commercial enterprises.

M.M. Long Livery Stable and Opera House
901 Congress Avenue
(c.1860)

M.M. Long operated the stage line from Austin to Burnet to Lampasas. While waiting for the stagecoach one could enjoy a concert at the opera house located on the second floor.

Millet Opera House
110 East 9th Street
(1878)

Architect Jacob Larmour designed this elegant building to be an opera house where singers such as Lillie Langtry graced the stage.

Eugene Bremond Building
801-803 Congress Avenue
(1886)

On this site stood a log cabin, which served as the business office of the Presidents of the Republic and the first four Governors of the State of Texas.

Site of the first Capitol of the Republic
Austin City Hall, 124 West 8th Street

A wood cabin was built on this site and served as the first Capitol of the Republic until 1853.

Johns-Hamilton Building
716 Congress Avenue
(1870)

This was the site of the log cabin offices of the Secretary of State and the Secretary of the Navy of the Republic of Texas.

Walter Tips Building
710-712 Congress Avenue
(1876)

Architect J.N. Preston designed this Venetian Gothic, three story building. The interior columns and girders are made of recast, exploded Confederate shells.

Paramount Theatre 472-5411
713 Congress Avenue
(1915)

Designed by architect George Endress and built for Ernest Nalle as the Majestic Theatre. Today it is considered one of the nation's most beautiful performing arts theatres.

Norwood Tower
114 West 7th Street
(1929)

This elegant Gothic Revival is straight out of a Batman movie set. When it was completed, it housed Austin's first parking garage and later was the first air conditioned office building in the United States.

Sampson-Henricks Building

620 Congress Avenue

(1859)

Another design by Abner Cook, this Italianate style structure served as the dry goods company of Sampson and Henricks.

Regents Plaza

West 6th & Colorado Streets

Enjoy free outdoor concerts at noon on Tuesdays during the spring and fall.

O Henry Hall

104 West 6th Street

(1881)

Originally served as the Post Office and Federal Building. This was the scene for the trial of short story writer, William Sydney Porter, better known as O Henry. When UT acquired the building in the 1960's, the name was changed to O Henry Hall.

> In 1898 Porter was tried and convicted of embezzling funds from Austin's First National bank.

Littlefield Building

601 Congress Avenue

(1910)

When the Littlefield Building was completed, it was the tallest building between New Orleans and San

Francisco. Built for Major George Washington Littlefield, a Civil War hero, banker and University of Texas benefactor, it originally was an eight story modern work of art. Not to be outdone, Littlefield added the ninth story after the eight story Scarbrough Building was constructed across the street.

Scarbrough Building
512-520 Congress Avenue
(1909)

E.M. Scarbrough began operating the finest department store in all of Texas at this location. The lot was sold for $2800 during the first land sale in Austin.

Driskill Hotel 474-5911
East 6th & Brazos Streets
(1886)
Tour: A self-guided walking tour map is available at the reception desk.

Take a step back in time as you enter this most elegant of Austin's hotels. Built for cattle baron Jesse Driskill, this has been the setting for lavish entertaining by the elite of Texas politics and business for over a century.

Robinson-Rosner
504 Congress Avenue
(1856)
The oldest known building on Congress Avenue.

Koppel Building
322 Congress Avenue
(1888)

This structure was built by William Radam who made a fortune with his patent medicine, "Microbe Killer."

> **Buford Tower &**
> **Kitchens Memorial Chimes**
> **(1930) 1st & Colorado**
>
> Until 1973 this served as a practice tower for the fire department. In 1978 the tower was restored and named in honor of Capt. James Buford who died in the line of duty.

Historic 6th Street

Jacoby Pope Building
200 East 6th Street
(1874)

This storefront design is typical of most commercial buildings of the time.

> **East 6th Street was the heart of the business community before the present Capitol was built on Congress Avenue**

Hannig Building
206 East 6th Street
(1875)

Designed by architect J.N. Preston for Joseph

Hannig, a cabinet maker and undertaker. This elegant building is a fine example of Victorian architecture. Hannig was married to Susanna Dickenson, a survivor of the Alamo.

Padgett-Warmath Building
208 East 6th Street
(1885)

Once a wholesale/retail saddlery and leather business, this is considered East 6th Street's most photogenic facade.

Platt-Simpson
310 East 6th Street
(1871)

This was a livery stable owned by Radcliff Platt. J.S. Simpson purchased the building in 1882 and opened a hardware store.

St. Charles House
316 East 6th Street
(1871)

This was the residence and store of Seba Bogart Brush, an Austin pioneer and merchant. In 1886, Madam Saffroni began operating a hotel and restaurant.

Dos Banderas
410 East 6th Street
(1881)

This was William Thaison's Saloon and Billiard Parlor. To look at this quaint townhouse today, you would never know that in 1961 it was condemned by the city for "nefarious activities within its portals."

In 1968, a local architect restored this as a townhouse and thus began the Sixth Street Restoration Project.

Quast Building
412 East 6th Street
(1872)

Take note of the distinctive roof garden and iron work. This served as the Quast residence.

Carrington Store
522 East 6th Street
(1880)

From 1872 to 1907 Edward Carrington, an African American merchant, operated a general store at this location. His son-in-law, Louis Lyons took over and continued as L.D. Lyons Fancy Groceries until the mid 1940's. Because of his benevolence and leadership in the African American community, Lyons was known as "the Black Mayor of 6th Street."

Paggi Carriage Shop
421 East 6th Street
(1875)

This was the Studebaker carriage and wagon

dealership of Michael Paggi. There was a proposal for a market square to be built to the south, so the rear of the shop was designed to be as attractive as the front. Paggi is also known as the man who brought the first ice machine to Austin.

Hamilton Building
419 East 6th Street
(1885)

Morgan Hamilton was Secretary of War for the Republic. His brother was Andrew Jackson Hamilton, the first provisional governor following the Civil War.

Cotton Exchange Building
401 East 6th Street
(1875)

The building gets its name from a cotton compress business that was located here.

Smith-Hage Building
325 East 6th Street
(1873)

Another example of Victorian Architecture, this structure served as McCormick's grocery store.

Morley-Grove Drug Store
209 East 6th Street
(1874)

This was a real drug store complete with a soda

fountain on the first floor. The Morley brothers were the first to occupy this building where they made and sold their patent medicines.

Historic Parks

Waterloo Park

East 15th Street to East 11th Street between Trinity and Red River

Waller Creek, once the eastern boundary of the city, is the focal point of this beautiful urban park. The land once was a vital part of the city with more than fifty buildings. Today it provides a place for concerts, children's parties or leisurely walks.

Brush Square

East 4th Street & Trinity

This park was named for Seba Bogart Brush, an Austin pioneer.

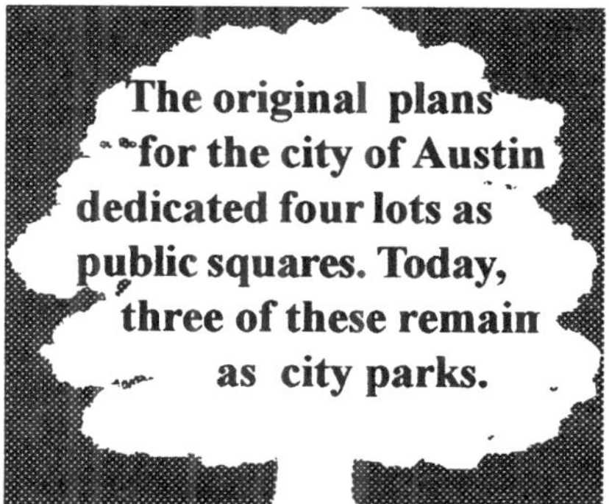

Republic Square

West 5th Street & Guadalupe

This was the site of Austin's first public land sale. On August 1, 1839, by order of the Congress of the Republic of Texas, Edwin Waller sold 306 lots for a total of $182,000.

Wooldridge Park

West 9th Street & Guadalupe

This block wasn't developed into a park until 1909. It is named for the first President of the Austin School Board and former mayor, A.P. Wooldridge.

Pease Park

1100 Kingsbury

Former Governor Elisha Pease donated 12 acres of his plantation along Shoal Creek to the city. It wasn't until 1913 that the area was developed into a park.

Treaty Oak

503 Baylor Street

This 600 year old oak tree, once considered the best specimen of a tree in North America, was part of a grove of trees known as Council Oaks. According to legend, Stephen F. Austin signed a treaty with the Indians under its majestic branches. In 1939 Austinites purchased the tree for $1000 to save it from land developers. The money was raised by bake sales and children donated their milk money. In 1989 the once proud tree was poisoned and valiant efforts were made to save it. Today only one crown remains.

Mt. Bonnell

Mt. Bonnell Road

1 mile past the end of West 35th Street

Climb the 99 steps to the highest point in the

Austin city limits, for a spectacular view of Lake Austin and the surrounding hills. This has been a popular spot for picnics and outings since the 1850's.

Capital of Texas Hwy. Bridge

Spans Lake Austin on Loop 360
(1982)

Officially named the Percy V. Pennybacker, Jr. Bridge, this is a great example of how Austinites have worked to blend progress with nature. The bluffs overlooking the bridge offer a natural setting for picnickers, hikers, rappellers and photographers. Next time you find yourself traveling Loop 360 take a minute to hike up the trail and experience the view.

Bats 327-9721

Bat Hotline .... 416-5700, Ext. 3636
Congress Avenue Bridge

The largest urban bat colony in North America lives under the Congress Avenue Bridge. From March until November they set up camp on the 1.5x16 inch spaces. It is quite a spectacular sight to see an estimated 1.5 million Mexican free tail bats emerge enmasse and fly into the night in search of insects.

The bats emerge from the east side of the bridge flying away from the setting sun. Depending on the time of year and the weather, they usually begin their flight about 30 minutes before sunset.

Zilker Park/Barton Springs

2100 Barton Springs Road

In 1832 William Barton settled on this land outside the settlement of Waterloo. Ownership changed hands several times; at the turn of the century Andrew Jackson Zilker acquired Barton Springs and the surrounding land. In 1918 Zilker donated the land the citizens of Austin with the stipulation that improvements be made to the Austin schools.

Zilker Park Attractions

Park Hours: 5am-10pm

Barton Springs Pool 867-3080

Hours: Open year round, subject to closure during and after a heavy rain)
Closed Thursdays from 9am to 7pm

Admission: Adult: weekdays $2.50; weekends $2.75
75 cents for ages 12-17;
50 cents for ages 11 and under

This natural spring fed pool is Austin's premier recreational attraction. Several million gallons of water flow from the spring each day. The springs create a pool over an eighth of a mile long with a year round temperature of a chilling 68 degrees.

Athletic Fields 480-3036

Call to reserve a field

8 Soccer fields; 2 Softball fields; 1 Rugby field

Nine hole Disc Golf Course. Baskets pulled in wet weather

Canoe Rental **478-3852**

Hours: October-March weekends only;
Summer 11am-dusk, daily

Zilker Eagle Train **478-8167**

Hours: Open year round 10am-dusk

Admission: Adult $1.25; Children $1.00

Gardens

National Wildflower Research Center

4801 La Crosse Avenue **282-4100**

Hours: Tuesday-Sunday 9am-5:30pm;
Closed: Holidays

Admission: $3.50 adults;
$2.00 students and senior citizens
$1.00 children 18 months to 5 years

Founded in 1982 by Lady Bird Johnson for the study, preservation and reestablishment of North American native plants. The Wildlife Center is a unique combination of gardens and natural spaces. You can hike on the nature trail winding through the wildflower meadow; enjoy the beauty of the formal courtyard or take a side trip to the wildflower cave.

Mayfield Park 499-6700

3801 West 35th Street

Hours: 5am-10pm daily

Mayfield Park sits on 23 acres overlooking the Colorado River. It consists of a magnificent two acre formal garden of native plants, graceful palm trees, rock gardens and lily ponds surrounded by a nature preserve. This wonderful resource of native plants and diverse landscaping was developed by Milton and Mary Mayfield Gutsch with their partner Esteban Arredondo in the 1920's and 1930's. Today it is operated by the Austin Parks and Recreation Department.

Zilker Park Botanical Gardens 477-8672
Hours: Daylight-Dark, daily
Admission: Free

Take a leisurely stroll through the roses, or spend a quiet moment meditating in the Japanese Garden.

Historic Churches

St. Mary's Cathedral 476-6182
10th & Brazos Streets
(1874)

Designed by architect Nicholas Clayton. This is the oldest Catholic Church in Austin. The cathedral, built in the shape of the Latin cross, is famous for its massive Gothic doorway, and rose window.

St. David's Episcopal Church 472-1196
7th & San Jacinto Blvd.
(1854)

It is thought to be the oldest Protestant church west of the Mississippi. Some of the stained glass windows were designed by Tiffany. St. David's was also known as the "Gambler's Church" because money to build the church came from local gamblers.

Gethsemane Lutheran Church

16th & Congress Avenue

(1883)

This was the first Lutheran Church in Travis County. Stones from the capitol, which burned in 1881, were hauled in wheelbarrows for the construction. The ornate panelled doors came from the Old Main Building at the University of Texas.

Historic Cemeteries

Oakwood Cemetery 475-4167

16th Street & Navasota

(1839)

The oldest cemetery in the city provides the final resting place for the early settlers and founders of Austin, as well as Governors of Texas and their families.

Goodrich Cemetery

2107 Goodrich Avenue

Established in the 1860's as a burial place for slaves, it was part of the Goodrich Plantation.

Texas State Cemetery 463-0605

909 Navasota
(1851)

Hours: Grounds: 8am-5pm everyday
Visitors Center: 8am-5pm Monday-Saturday
Tours: Upon request, call for reservation
Admission: Free

The State Cemetery, known as the Arlington of Texas, provides a final resting place for the men and women who dedicated their lives for this great state. You can pay your respects at the gravesites of Texas Governors, American War Veterans, Republic of Texas and Confederate War Veterans.

Texas history comes to life as you read the names of such notables as Stephen F. Austin, the Father of Texas, Joanna Troutman, designer of the Texas battleflag, John Connally, Governor of Texas, Barbara Jordan, U.S. Representative.

Burial Eligibility

Members or former members of the Texas Legislature

Elected state officials or state officials appointed by the Governor and confirmed by the Senate

Persons designated by Governor's Proclamation or a Concurrent Resolution of the legislature and approved by the State Cemetery Committee

Persons who have made a significant contribution to Texas culture and history as determined by the State Cemetery Committee

Confederate Veterans

The Spouses of anyone meeting these criteria

Historic Neighborhoods & Homes

Waterloo Compound

East 3rd & Red River

(1854)

In 1854, the two story stone building on the corner was constructed by J. Henry Hofheintz, as a grocery and dry goods store. It is one of the oldest commercial buildings in Austin, and remained an active grocery store until 1954. The buildings are on land which was part of the original community of Waterloo.

French Legation Museum

802 San Marcos Street

(1841)

Hours: Tuesday-Sunday 1pm-5pm

Admission: $3.00 adults, $2.00 senior citizens, $1.00 children

This lovingly maintained frame cottage is Austin's oldest known building. When France recognized the Republic of Texas as a nation they sent Alphonse Dubois de Saligny to establish the French Legation. In 1848 the house was purchased by the Dr. Joseph W. Robertson family and served as their homestead until 1949 when the family sold it to the state. Today it is maintained by the Daughters of the Republic of Texas.

Symphony Square

11th Street & Red River

(1881-1887)

This is a complex of four 100 year old buildings. The Jeremiah Hamilton Building is one of three stone triangular buildings still standing in Texas. Today it serves as the offices for the Austin Symphony. The square also contains the Michael Doyle House, the New Orleans Club Mercantile, and the Hardeman House.

Bremond Block

7th & 8th Streets; San Antonio & Guadalupe
(1853-1857)

The Bremond Block gives us a glimpse of the grandeur and opulence that was present in Austin during the mid 1800's. These homes were built, remodeled and lived in by one of Austin's early, successful merchant and banking families, the Bremonds. Since the homes were built on a square block, their backyards provided a playground for the family's many children. Today these homes are not open to the public, but a stroll around the block will take you back to a time when Austin's downtown district was a thriving residential neighborhood.

North-Evans Chateau

708 San Antonio
(1874-1892)

Harvey and Catherine North came to Austin from New Orleans where Harvey had been a successful merchant. Their new home, influenced by their trips to Europe, rivaled the grandeur of the Bremond homes.

Unfortunately the Norths' experienced a reversal of fortunes and had to sell the house for half the cost. In 1929 the chateau became the headquarters for the Austin Women's Club.

Carrington-Covert House
1511 Colorado
(1857)

Leonidas Carrington, owner of a large mercantile store on Congress Avenue, paid $985.95 to have this house built. When it was completed it was considered the largest home in Austin. Saved from demolition for a parking lot in the 1960's, today it serves as the administration offices of the Texas Heritage Commission.

Caswell House
1404 West Avenue
(1900)

This elegant Victorian mansion was built at the turn of the century and quite unique with electrical lighting and indoor running water. This was the home of D. H. Caswell who made his fortune in cotton. His son, D.H. Caswell, Jr. was instrumental in establishing the Parks and Recreation Department.

Pease Mansion
6 Niles Road
(1853)

This Greek Revival style mansion was designed by Abner Cook for James B. Shaw. In 1857 it was purchased by Elisha M. Pease, the first governor to reside in the Governor's Mansion. The property was extensive and included the land which today is Pease Park. It is said that Pease donated some of his estate land to freed men after the Civil War for the settlement of the Clarksville District.

Clarksville Historic District

Mopac & West Lynn; 10th & Waterson Streets

In 1871, freed man Charles Griffith Clark bought two acres of land and developed a neighborhood where other African Americans could live and create a community of their own. This area takes in parts of 11 blocks and contains 90 small frame houses.

Laguna Gloria
Austin Museum of Art 458-8191

3809 West 35th Street

(1915)

Hours: Tuesday-Saturday 10am-5pm; Thursday 10am-9pm; Sunday 1pm-5pm; Closed Mondays and holidays

Admission: Adults $2.00
Students & Senior Visitors $1.00
Thursdays are free of charge

Built on land once owned by Stephen F. Austin, this Mediterranean style villa was built for Clara Discoll

Sevier, a successful banker and businesswoman. In 1903 Clara saved the Alamo from commercial development by purchasing the property and donating it to the state of Texas.

Formosa, Elisabet Ney Studio

304 East 44th Street
(1892)
Hours: Wednesday-Saturday 10am-5pm; Sunday 12pm-5pm
Admission: Free

Nestled on the edge of Hyde Park, it is one of Austin's most interesting buildings. It was designed by sculptor Elisabet Ney as her studio and home. The studio has a wall that opens on the rear of the house to facilitate moving large pieces of sculpture. The Gothic tower was added as a study for her husband Dr. Edmund Montgomery. Stairs lead from the studio to the roof where Ney preferred to sleep in a hammock to star gaze and perhaps find relief from the Texas heat.

Hyde Park

39th to 45th Streets; Avenue B to Avenue H
(1890)

Entrepreneur Monroe Shipe purchased this tract of land in far north Austin to develop into a middle class neighborhood. Today it serves as a sampler of American architectural styles.

Neill-Cochran House
2310 San Gabriel
(1855)
Hours: Wednesday-Sunday 2pm-5pm
Admission: $2.00

Designed by Abner Cook this is considered a perfect example of the Texas Greek Revival Style. When the house was built for Washington L. Hill, the property included 40 acres which extended west to Shoal Creek. Hill's wife, fearing Indian attacks, refused to live in the house, so in 1856 it became the original institute for the blind. During the last months of the Civil War it served as a hospital for Union soldiers. The house was sold to Andrew Neill in 1876. T.B. Cochran purchased the house in 1895.

The University of Texas

Little Campus
Red River & Martin Luther King Blvd.
(1857-1891)

Originally built as the State Blind Asylum. In 1865 George Armstrong Custer occupied the building when he came to Texas to support Reconstruction. The University of Texas acquired this complex in 1925.

Santa Rita #1
Trinity and Martin Luther King Blvd.
(1921)

This little rig could be considered the most

important piece of property the University ever owned.

On May 23, 1923 the Santa Rita brought in the first oil on university owned land in west Texas. Since that day almost two billion dollars in royalties have been shared by UT and Texas A&M. With the split of the profits being UT two-thirds, A&M one-third, it makes you wonder if football is the real rivalry.

Littlefield House

24th Street & Whitis

(1893)

George Washington Littlefield made his living as a banker and cattleman. He made considerable donations to the University of Texas. Today this lovely Victorian house is owned by the University and is used for special functions as well as office space.

Littlefield Fountain

21st Street & University

(1932)

A memorial to UT students who served in World War I.

LBJ Presidential Library & Museum 916-5137

2313 Red River

Hours: Open everyday except Christmas 9am-5pm

Admission: Free

Parking: Park free in the library parking

Don't expect to find piles of dusty papers here!

This library and museum is state of the art with videos and sound to enhance the exhibits. The 1st, 2nd and 8th floors have permanent exhibits featuring the life and political career of Lyndon Johnson. Exhibits include: A replica of the Oval Office; hand made gifts from the American people for their President; gifts LBJ received from foreign countries; a history of the 1960's; The Family Album, a pictorial history of LBJ's life from 1908 until his death in 1973; The First Lady Theatre which contains portraits of all the first ladies of the United States.

On the 3rd through 6th floors you will find the archives containing the political papers of LBJ's political career as a U.S. Congressman, U.S. Senator, Vice President and President. This is also the repository for the papers of Lady Bird Johnson, John Connally, General Westmoreland and Liz Carpenter.

Access to the archives is by appointment only,
Monday - Friday 9am-5pm

LBJ agreed to leave his papers to the University of Texas with the stipulation that they also build a School of Public Affairs. When the library was completed UT was the only university to house a Presidential Library.

Harry Ransom Center 471-8944
UT Campus
21st & Guadalupe
Hours: Monday-Saturday 9am-5pm;
Sunday 1pm-5pm
Admission: Free

This is UT Austin's internationally recognized rare book and manuscript library. Exhibits include the Michener Collection and the Gutenberg Bible.

Center for American History 495-4515
UT Campus
Sid Richardson Hall (adjacent to LBJ Library)
Hours: Monday-Saturday 9am-5pm

This is a special collections library, archives, and museum for programs on the historical development of the United States. The Barker Texas History Collection is the most extensive collection of Texas related material in existence.

The University of Texas Tower (1934-1935)

For years this symbol of the University of Texas dominated the Austin skyline as the tallest structure in the city. Today it houses the administrative offices and the office of the President of the University.

UT Tower Honor Lights

Tower orange with the #1 displayed on each side

1. On occasions marking great distinction in the life of The University.
2. When a NCAA national team championship is won in any approved varsity sport (excluding club sports).

Complete Tower Orange

1. At Commencement.
2. When a Big 12 Championship is won in any team sport.
3. On nights of football victories over Texas A&M.
4. When a basketball tournament championship is won in the NI or the NWIT.
5. On Honors Day, March 2, July 4.

Tower shaft white, observation and column decks orange

1. Football victories other than those involving Texas A&M.
2. For basketball or baseball victories in a Big 12 Tournament so long as the team is in the running for the national championship.
3. For victories in NCAA district or regional championships so long as the team is in the running for the national championship.
4. For each basketball victory in the NIT or NWIT.
5. On April 21, Easter, Memorial Day, Thanksgiving Day and Christmas Day.

Moonlight Towers

In 1895 Austin was bathed in artificial moonlight when 31 towers were illuminated for the first time. The electricity was generated by the dam which was built across the Colorado River in 1890. Because of the hills the 165 foot towers, each lighting 4 square blocks, were preferred to other lighting systems of the time. Seventeen of the original 31 towers still provide Austin with artificial moonlight.

Locations

West 12th and Blanco Streets
West 12th and Rio Grande Streets
South 1st and Monroe Streets
Martin Luther King, Jr. Blvd. and Chicon Street
West 9th and Guadalupe Streets
Canterbury and Lynn Streets
22nd and Nueces Streets
East 13th and Coleto Streets
East 11th and Lydia Streets
East 11th and Trinity Streets
Trinity and Cesar Chavez Streets
East Side Drive and Leland Street
West 15th and San Antonio Streets
Speedway and 41st Street
Leona and Pennsylvania Streets
West 4th and Nueces Streets
Zilker Park

Museums

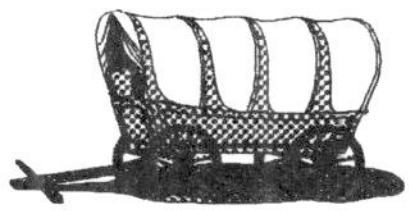

Austin Children's Museum 472-2499
1501 West 5th Street
Hours: Tuesday-Saturday 10am-5pm,
Sunday 12pm-5pm
Admission: $2.50 adults and children,
Free for children under age 2
Hands-on exhibits for children and families.

Austin History Center 499-7480
810 Guadalupe
Hours: Monday-Thursday 9am-9pm;
Friday-Saturday 9am-6pm;
Sunday 12pm-6pm
Admission: Free

This Renaissance Revival building originally served as the Austin main library. Today it houses the archives of Austin and Travis County history. You can access old photographs and drawings of Austin; see historical exhibits; browse through books and documents on Austin and Travis County.

George Washington Carver 472-4809
1165 Angelina Street
Hours: Tuesday-Thursday 10am-6pm;
Friday-Saturday 12pm-5pm;
Closed Sunday and Monday
Admission: Free

The Carver Museum was the first African American neighborhood museum in Texas. A proud African American heritage is showcased by rotating special exhibitions of artists and significant historical events.

French Legation Museum 472-8180
(1841) 802 San Marcos Street
Hours: Tuesday-Sunday 1pm-5pm
Admission: $3.00 adults, $2.00 Senior Visitors, $1.00 children

In 1839 France officially recognized the Republic of Texas. Alphonse Dubois de Saligny was named charge d'affaires and in 1840 he arrived to establish the French Legation. In 1848 the house was purchased by the Dr. Joseph W. Robertson family and served as their homestead until 1949 when the family sold it to the state. The Daughters of the Republic of Texas have restored the house and outbuildings to their original designs. The parlor contains some furnishings that belonged to de Saligny; others are period pieces. The Legation's kitchen is the only authentic reproduction of an early Creole kitchen in the United States.

"The Pig War"

de Saligny provided a much needed comic relief to the harsh life of early Austin. He was pretentious to say the least, arriving by ox cart with elegant clothes, fancy dishes and linens. Unfortunately for the Count,

Austin was a town of log cabins, dirt roads, cowboys and pigs. During the construction of the legation, he lived in a temporary residence on 6th Street, where a neighbor's pigs broke in and ate some of his linens and diplomatic papers. He retaliated by killing the pigs; the pig owner retaliated by beating the Count and his servant. de Saligny demanded retribution by International Law. When this was refused he left town, after living in the completed legation for a mere 6 weeks. de Saligny did have his revenge. Although France thought this whole affair ridiculous, they did refuse a much needed loan to the new Republic.

Jordan-Bachman Pioneer Farm 837-1215

11418 Sprinkle Cut Off Road

Hours: Sundays 1pm-5pm
June-August, Monday-Thursday 9:30am-3pm
September-May, Monday-Wednesday 9:30am-1:00pm

Admission: $3.00 adults; $2.00 children

Sitting on the edge of Austin's city limits is a farming community that represents life in rural central Texas in the 1880's. Interpreters, dressed in period clothing, demonstrate the skills that were necessary to survive. Three families representing different economic and ethnic backgrounds are portrayed.

Visit in the fall and help pick cotton, then see it spun into yarn. Experience the sights and smells of cooking in a wood-burning stove or on an open fire. Day camps are available for children and adults; learn the work and play of farm life in the 1880's while dressed in period clothing.

Mexic-Arte Museum 480-9373

419 Congress Avenue
Hours: Monday-Saturday 10am-6pm
Admission: $2.00 suggested donation

Through collections of photographs, prints and artifacts, this museum is dedicated to the promotion and development of multi-cultural artistic expression.

Neill-Cochran House 478-2335

(1855) 2310 San Gabriel
Hours: Wednesday-Sunday 2pm-5pm
Admission: $2.00

Take a step back in time as you enter this elegant mansion. Each room is furnished with period pieces of the 19th century. Designed by Abner Cook it is considered a perfect example of the Texas Greek Revival.

In 1865 General Custer and his Union Calvary came to Texas to support Reconstruction. He took possession of the Neill-Cochran House and used it as his headquarters. It was also used as a hospital for Union soldiers.

Elisabet Ney Museum 458-2255

304 East 44th Street

Hours: Wednesday-Saturday 10am-5pm; Sunday 12pm-5pm

Admission: Free

Born in Germany in 1833, Elisabet Ney immortalized in stone notables from Europe to Texas. In the 1870's Ney moved to Texas with her husband, Dr. Edmund Montgomery, where they settled on a plantation near Hempstead. At the age of 59, Ney moved to Austin and built her studio in Hyde Park. She was commissioned by the State of Texas to sculpt statues of Stephen F. Austin and Sam Houston for the state capitol.

Elisabet Ney was a pioneer in the artistic development of Texas. A colorful and influential woman, she was a fierce advocate of the arts. In her memory friends established the Texas Fine Arts Association and the Texas Commission on the Arts.

O. Henry Museum 472-1903

409 East 5th Street

(1881)

Hours: Wednesday-Sunday 12pm-5pm

Admission: Free

This little cottage was the residence of short story writer William Sydney Porter. He lived in Austin from 1884 until 1895, when he took a job with the Houston Post. During his years here he worked in a drug store; was a real estate agent; worked as a draftsman in the Old Land Office; was a teller in the First National Bank; and published a newspaper called the "Rolling Stone."

Republic of Texas Museum...............339-1997
510 East Anderson Lane
Hours: Monday-Friday 10am-4pm
Admission: $2.00 adults; $1.50 senior citizens; Students 50 cents

This museum is dedicated to the perpetuation and preservation of the memory and spirit of the men and women who achieved and maintained the independence of Texas.

Texas Memorial Museum...............471-1605
2400 Trinity
Hours: Monday-Friday 9am-5pm
Saturday 10am-5pm; Sunday 1pm-5pm
Admission: Free

Exhibits include dinosaur bones and footprints; life-size dioramas of Texas wild life; habitats of native birds; displays of Texas' poisonous and harmless reptiles. There is also a series of exhibits highlighting the major native North American cultural groups.

"The Mustangs"
The group of seven plunging mustangs, at the base of the west steps on San Jacinto Blvd.,represent the "spirited horses that carried the men that made Texas."

Texas Military Forces Museum 406-6967
Camp Mabry,
3500 West 35th Street
Hours: Wednesday 10am-4pm;
Thursday-Sunday 2pm-6pm
Admission: Free

A museum and archival collection , dedicated to the men and women who served in the military forces of Texas, was opened in 1992. Exhibits include dioramas of the Alamo and the Taking of Velettri by the 36th Division in World War II. Also on display are memorabilia, photographs, flags, uniforms and military weapons from the Texas Revolution to Desert Storm.

The Chapel on the grounds of Camp Mabry has stained glass windows depicting the battles of the Republic of Texas

Umlauf Museum.............................455-5582
605 Robert E. Lee Road
Hours: Friday & Saturday 10am-4:30pm
Thursday & Sunday 1pm-4:30pm
Admission: $2.00 adults; $1.00 students;
Children under age six free

See 130 pieces of sculpture by Charles Umlauf. His work varies from the realistic to the abstract; his materials from wood and cast stone to bronze and marble.

That's Entertainment

There is always something live going on!
Whether it be music, theatre, or dance.
From classical to grunge.
Austin's got it.

Big Ticket Events

Advance tickets are usually required for performances at the following locations:

The Frank Erwin Center **477-6060**
1701 Red River
UT Performing Arts Center **471-1444**
23rd & East Campus Drive
Paramount Theatre **472-5411**
713 Congress Avenue
Austin Music Hall **263-4146**
Third & Nueces
The Backyard **263-4146**
13101 Texas 71 West
Southpark Meadows **280-8771**
9600 South IH-35

Visabands **477-6060**

If you're willing to stand in line, you will need a visa band to buy tickets for the really big shows at the Erwin Center. These can be obtained at all H.E.B. Stores or the Erwin Center on the date announced by local radio stations. The band indicates what number in line you will be when you return to the same location on the day of the ticket sales. You must pay cash and show a picture I.D.

UTTM **477-6060**

University of Texas Ticket Master offers tickets for Erwin Center events which do not require a visa band, Paramount Theatre presentations and other UT productions. Tickets can also be purchased by phone.

UTTM Ticket Centers

The Frank Erwin Center
1701 Red River
Performing Arts Center
23rd & East Campus Drive
Texas Union
Guadalupe at 24th Street

Paramount Theatre
713 Congress Avenue
H.E.B. Stores in Austin, Round Rock, Cedar Park, Pflugerville, Georgetown

Star Tickets **469-7469**

Star Tickets sells tickets for the events at Southpark Meadows, the Austin Music Hall, Stubbs` and the Backyard. You may purchase tickets by phone or at one of their ticket outlets.

PAC **471-1444**

23rd & East Campus Drive

The Performing Arts Center at UT handles the sale of tickets for events at Bass Concert Hall, Bates Recital Hall, McCullough Theatre and Payne Theatre.

AusTix **320-7168**

Dougherty Arts Center, 1110 Barton Springs Rd.

Hours: Wednesday-Friday 11:30am-6:30pm;
Saturday 11am-2pm

Visitors Center, 201 East 2nd Street

Hours: Thursday-Saturday 11:30am-1:30pm

Offers half-price, day of performance tickets for various live entertainment events throughout Austin.

Clubs and Coffeehouses

A sampling of Austin's live music venues.

Antone's **320-8424**
213 West 5th Street **Genre**: Blues, Rock

Antonio's Cantina **238-8969**
14735 Bratton Lane **Genre**: Blues, Jazz, Rock

Antonio's Cantina **257-2144**
11835 Jollyville Road **Genre**: Blues, Jazz, Rock

Artz Rib House **442-8283**
2230 South Lamar **Genre**: Folk; Bluegrass, Singer, Songwriter

Austin Music Hall **263-4146**
West 3rd and Nueces Streets **Genre**: Touring Shows

Babe's **473-2262**
208 East 6th Street **Genre**: Blues, Rock, Country

Back Room **441-4677**
2015 East Riverside Drive **Genre**: Rock

Backyard **263-4146**
13101 Highway 71 West **Genre**: Touring Shows

Bates Motel **480-8121**
317 East 6th Street **Genre**: Punk

Bitter End **478-2337**
311 Colorado Street **Genre**: R&B

Blondie's **472-7343**
510 Rio Grande **Genre**: Alternative

Bob Popular **478-3352**
402 East 6th Street **Genre**: Rock and Pop

Boomerz **892-3358**
6148 U.S.290 West **Genre**: Country

Broken Spoke **442-6189**
3201 South Lamar **Genre**: Country

Cactus Cafe **475-6515**
Texas Union, UT **Genre**: Blues, Singer, Songwriter, Bluegrass

Carlos 'N' Charlies **266-1683**
5973 Hi Line Road **Genre**: Eclectic, Blues, Rock

Caucus Club **472-2873**
912 Red River Street **Genre**: Jazz

Cedar Street Courtyard **495-9669**
208 West 4th Street **Genre**: Live Jazz 7 nights a week

Armadillo World Headquarters

The single most important influence on the Austin music scene was the Armadillo World Headquarters. This laid back music hall, located in a renovated skating rink on the corner of Barton Springs Road and Riverside Drive, served the music community from 1970 to 1980.

The Armadillo provided a venue for known artists, B.B. King, Willie Nelson and Jerry Lee Lewis; as well as struggling talents, Bruce Springsteen, Frank Zappa, ZZ Top, Commander Cody and the Lost Planet Airmen, just to name a few. Although the building is gone, the spirit lives on in the hearts of music lovers. Austin now rivals Nashville, Los Angeles and New York City with live entertainment by local and guest performers every night of the week.

Central Market Cafe **206-1000**
4001 North Lamar **Genre:** Jazz, Lounge, Acoutics, Pop

Chaparral Lounge **441-9008**
5500 South Congress Avenue **Genre:** Country

Club Flamingo **243-1188**
8619 Highway 183 South **Genre:** Tejano

Continental Club **441-2444**
1315 South Congress Avenue **Genre:** Blues, Rock, Country

Copper Tank **478-8444**
504 Trinity Street **Genre:** Rock

Dance Across Texas **441-9101**
2201 East Ben White **Genre:** Country

Dessau Music Hall **252-1123**
13422 Dessau **Genre:** Country

Donn's Depot **478-0336**
1600 West 5th Street **Genre:** Country

Draught Horse Pub **452-6258**
4112 Medical Parkway **Genre:** Country

Driskill Hotel Bar **474-5911**
604 Brazos **Genre:** Piano

Ego's **474-7091**
510 South Congress Avenue **Genre:** Lounge, Piano, Jazz

Electric Lounge **476-3873**
302 Bowie Street **Genre:** Alternative

Elephant Room **473-2279**
315 Congress Avenue **Genre:** Jazz

Emo's **477-3667**
603 Red River Street **Genre:** Alternative

Flamingo Cantina **474-9336**
515 East 6th Street **Genre:** Reggae, Punk

Flipnotics Coffeespace **322-9750**
1601 Barton Springs **Genre:** Rockabilly, Acoustic, Blues,

Giddyup's **280-4732**
12000 Manchaca Road **Genre:** Country

Gilligan's **474-7474**
407 Colorado **Genre:** Jazz

Hole in the Wall **472-5599**
2538 Guadalupe Street **Genre:** Original Austin Rock

Iron Cactus **472-9240**
606 Trinity **Genre:** Jazz

Jazz on Sixth Street **479-0474**
212 East 6th Street **Genre:** Jazz

Joe's Generic Bar **480-0171**
315 East 6th Street **Genre:** Blues

La Calle Ocho **320-0658**
706 Congress Avenue **Genre:** Latin

La Zona Rosa **472-2293**
612 West 4th Street **Genre:** Eclectic mix of Austin

Liberty Lunch **477-0461**
405 West 2nd Street **Genre:** Touring Shows

Lucy's Retired Surfer's Bar **472-7873**
219 East 6th Street **Genre**: Rock

Maggie Mae's **478-8541**
323 East 6th Street **Genre**: Cover bands playing top 40's music

Mama Mia's **451-0177**
8015 Shoal Creek Blvd. **Genre**: Piano

The Mercury **457-0706**
503 East 6th Street **Genre**: Alternative

The Oasis **266-2442**
6550 Comanche Trail **Genre**: Varied

Pearl's Oyster Bar **339-7444**
9033 Research Blvd. **Genre**: R&B, Pop

The Pier **327-4562**
1703 River Hills Road **Genre**: Rock, Varied

Rascals **246-7979**
3103 South IH-35 **Genre**: Country

Ritz Lounge **474-2270**
302 East 6th Street **Genre**: Latin

Ruta Maya Coffee House **472-9637**
218 West 4th Street **Genre**: Acoustic

The Saloon **442-8885**
1502 West Ben White **Genre**: Country

Saxon Pub **448-2552**
1320 South Lamar **Genre**: R&B, Country, Varied

Speakeasy **476-8017**
412 Congress Avenue **Genre**: Swing

Steamboat **478-2913**
403 East 6th Street **Genre**: Rock

Stubb's Bar-B-Q **480-8341**
801 Red River **Genre**: Blues, Rock

Sullivans **478-1870**
300 Colorado Street **Genre**: Jazz

Tejano Ranch **453-6615**
7601 North Lamar **Genre**: Tejano

Top of the Marc **472-9849**
618 West 6th Street **Genre**: Varied

Victory Grill **474-4494**
1104 East 11th Street **Genre**: Jazz

SXSW

The largest showcase of popular music in the country is the South by Southwest Music, Film and Multimedia Festival held each year in March. It is an exciting nine day event for live entertainment lovers. Over 30 clubs with 7 bands a night vie for attention at this musical extravaganza.

For ticket information call:
467-7979

Austin City Limits Tapings

KLRU Studio
UT Campus, Communications Building B
26th & Guadalupe

This innovative show, spotlighting the music scene in Austin, has become the longest running popular music series on television. The show is taped at the KLRU Studio on the UT Campus.

To obtain tickets to a taping follow these steps:
1. Call Austin City Limits **HOTLINE**...... **475-9077**

2. The recorded message will give the artist, taping date, time, and which radio station to listen to for the tickets distribution announcement.

3. The radio station will announce what time the tickets will be given away, usually within the hour. This could be in the morning or the afternoon.

4. When you hear the announcement come to KLRU **IMMEDIATELY** for ticket distribution.

Tickets are distributed by KLRU staff
They are free on a first come, first served basis
Two tickets per person allowed

On taping day **ARRIVE EARLY**, admission is not guaranteed. KLRU strives to admit every ticket holder for every taping. Fire codes limit capacity to 400 audience members, but in order to be assured of a full house for the taping KLRU distributes an excess of 400 tickets to account for those who fail to show.

The Performing Arts

Austin Lyric Opera **472-5927**
Austin's professional opera

Austin Musical Theatre **292-9696**
Paramount Theatre
Presents Broadway musicals

Austin Symphony Orchestra **476-6064**
Box Office: Symphony Square, 11th & Red River
Box Office Hours: Monday-Friday 9:00am-5:00pm
Performs year round in UT's Bass Concert Hall

Ballet Austin **476-9051**
UT Performing Arts Center
Austin's professional ballet company

Zilker Theatre Productions **479-9491**
Zilker Park
Performs outdoor musicals

Comedy

Capitol City Comedy Club **467-2333**
8120 Research Blvd.
Esther's Pool **320-0553**
525 East 6th Street
Velveeta Room **469-9116**
521 East 6th Street

Professional Theatres

Capitol City Playhouse **472-1855**
214 West 4th Street

Hyde Park Theatre **452-6688**
511 West 43rd Street

Live Oak Theatre **472-5143**
719 Congress Avenue

Paramount Theatre **472-5411**
713 Congress Avenue

The Public Domain **474-6202**
807 Congress Avenue

Sam Bass Theatre **244-0440**
Round Rock

Santa Cruz Center **478-9311**
1805 East 7th Street

Zachary Scott Theatre **476-0541**
1510 Toomey Road

Zilker Hillside Theatre **397-1463**
Zilker Park

University Theatres

UT Performing Arts Center **471-1444**
UT Campus, 23rd Street & East Campus Drive
Bass Concert Hall: Ballet Austin, Austin Symphony, Touring Shows
Bates Recital Center: Dance and music recitals
McCullough Theatre: Dance and opera performances
Payne Theatre: UT's drama theatre

St. Edward's University **448-8484**
Mary Moody Northern Theatre

Austin Community College **223-3246**
1212 Rio Grande

Concordia University 452-0666
Peter Center
Huston-Tillotson College 505-3000
900 Chicon Street
Southwestern University 512/863-1378
Jones Theatre, Georgetown, TX
Southwest Texas State 512/245-2204
San Marcos, TX

Movie Theatres

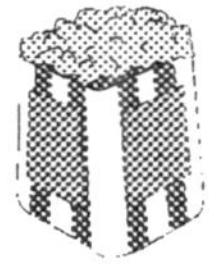

Alamo Drafthouse	409 Colorado Street	867-1839
Arbor	Arboretum	346-6937
Barton Creek Cinema	2224 Walsh Tarlton	306-1688
Discount Cinema 8	3407 Wells Branch Pkwy.	244-6622
Dobie Theatre	2021 Guadalupe Street	472-3456
Gateway	Research & 360	416-5700
Great Hills 8	9828 Great Hills Trail	794-8076
Highland Cinema	6700 Middle Fiskville	454-9562
Lake Creek	13729 Research	219-0291
Lakehills	13729 Ben White	444-0552
Lakeline Mall	Lakeline Mall	335-7138
Lincoln	6406 North IH-35	454-6469
Northcross	Northcross Mall	454-5147
Riverside	2410 East Riverside	448-0008
Round Rock 8	2120 Mays Street	388-2848
Show Place 6	10405 Lake Creek Pkwy.	258-7525
Tinseltown Austin	I-35 & Stassney Lane	326-3800
Tinseltown Pflugerville	15425 FM 1825	989-8540
Village Cinema	2700 Anderson Lane	451-8352
Westgate 3	4608 Westgate Blvd.	892-2775
Westgate 8	4521 Westgate Blvd.	892-2696

AM Radio Stations

KLBJ	590	News, talk, sports	836-0590
KIXL	970	Christian information radio	447-KIXL
KFIT	1060	Gospel music	328-1060
KTAE	1260	Country, easy listening	352-3631
KVET	1300	News, talk, U.T. Sports	390-LIVE
KHLB	1340	40's, 50's, 60's	830/693-5452
KJCE	1370	Contemporary	390-KJCE
KELG	1440	Tejano music in Spanish	453-1440
KFON	1490	All sports	390-KFON
KNEZ	1530	Tejano	473-3200
KTXZ	1560	Tejano music	390-5560

FM Radio Stations

KNLE	88.1	Christian music	837-8801
KAZI	88.7	Jazz, blues, talk	836-2887
KMFA	89.5	Classical music	476-5632
KUT	90.5	News; eclectic music	471-2345
KOOP	91.7	Co-op radio with KVRX	472-KOOP
KVRX	91.7	U.T. Student radio	495-KVRX
KKLB	92.5	Tejano music	390-5552
KAJZ	93.3	Jazz	390-5933
KLBJ	93.7	Rock 'n Roll	832-4094
KAMX	94.7	Adult contemporary	390-5947
KKMJ	95.5	Hits from '70s to '90s	390-KKMJ
KHFI	96.7	Contemporary hits	390-KHFI
KVET	98.1	Country music	390-KVET
KRXT	98.5	Country music	512/446-6985
KJFK	98.9	Rock; Howard Stern	390-5989
KASE	100.7	Country music	390-KASE
KROX	101.5	New rock alternative	390-KROX
KPEZ	102.3	Classic rock	390-5000
KEYI	103.5	Oldie '50's & '60's	390-5060
KHLB	106.9	Country	830/693-5452
KGSR	107.1	Blues, jazz, folk	390-KGSR
KAHK	107.7	Classic rock	390-KNAC
KFAN	107.9	Blues	210/997-2197

Television Stations

KTBC	Fox	Cable 2	UHF 7
KVUE	ABC	Cable 3	UHF 24
KXAN	NBC	Cable 4	UHF 36
KEYE	CBS	Cable 5	UHF 42
KLRU	PBS	Cable 9	UHF 18
KNVA	Independent	Cable 12	UHF 54
KVC	Independent	Cable 13	UHF 3
AMN	Music	Cable 15	UHF 9
ACTV	Local access	Cable 10,11,16	

Cable Companies

Time Warner Communications **485-5555**
Serves Austin, Lago Vista, West Lake Hills

Heartland Wireless **800-876-6299**
Austin and surrounding areas

CableVision of Lake Travis **263-9194**
Serves Lakeway and Lake Travis

CableVision **930-3085**
Serves Georgetown, Leander, Pflugerville

Get a Life

Use your imagination...
Take an art class

The world's a stage .... Be on it

Don't miss a beat ...
Take music lessons

Be part of a team

Play a sport

Get involved....
Volunteer

Community Schools

Austin and Round Rock Independent School Districts make full use of their campuses by holding informal classes during their off- hours. For children, this program includes an after school care program, tutoring, arts, sports and summer camps. Adults are offered a variety of courses too, from languages, to computers, to country western dancing.

AISD Campuses

Becker	**906 West Milton**	**442-0584**
Bedichek	**6800 Bill Hughes Road**	**441-8919**
Murchison	**3700 North Hills Drive**	**346-8930**
Webb	**601 East St. Johns Avenue**	**450-0914**

Round Rock ISD Campuses

Round Rock	**300 Lake Creek Drive**	**255-3450**
Westwood	**12400 Mellow Meadow**	**258-8224**

Dougherty Arts Center

1110 Barton Springs Road 397-1468

The Center offers a variety of visual and performing arts programs for all ages. The art school provides multi-disciplinary classes which include painting and drawing, photography, silkscreen, pottery, acting and dance.

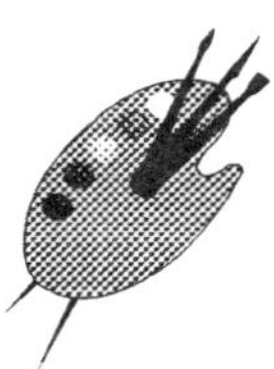

Art School at Laguna Gloria 458-8191
3809 West 35th Street

Children and adults alike will be able to express themselves through the variety of art classes offered at Laguna Gloria.

Elisabet Ney
Sculpture Conservatory 371-7606
East 45th Street (behind the museum)

The spirit and artistic technique of Elisabet Ney is kept alive through a variety of classes which are offered seasonally in clay, plaster, stone sculpture and drawing.

O Henry Writing Club
O Henry Museum 472-1903
409 East 5th Street

This award winning, literary arts education program encourages students to improve writing skills and reading comprehension utilizing O Henry's short stories.

Parks and Recreation Department

The PARD does an excellent job of designing programs to meet the interests of area residents. From the fine arts to organized sports leagues there is something for all age groups.

Austin Main Office 499-6700
Cedar Park 258-4121
Lakeway 261-8403
Pflugerville 251-5082
Round Rock 867-6442

Scouting

Boy Scouts of America 926-6363
Girl Scouts of America 453-7391
Campfire Boys & Girls 462-2777

YMCA

Austin

Main Office 476-6705
1100 West Cesar Chavez Street

Southwest Branch and Preschool 891-9622
6219 Oakclaire

North Park Family Branch 973-9622
9616 North Lamar

East Program Center 476-1183
1809 East 6th Street

After School Child Care Program 476-1183
1809 East 6th Street

Williamson County

Hill Country Family Branch 250-9622
200 Buttercup Creek Blvd.

Round Rock Family Branch 244-1232
1812 North Mays

After School Care 244-1232
1812 North Mays

Swimming Pools

Austin City Pools

Call for information on hours and entrance fees

Bartholomew **928-0014**
1800 East 51st Street

Deep Eddy **472-8546**
401 Deep Eddy Avenue

Garrison **441-2772**
6001 Manchaca Road

Mabel Davis **441-5247**
3427 Parker Lane

Northwest **453-0194**
7000 Ardath Street

Walnut Creek **834-0824**
12138 North Lamar Blvd.

Barton Springs Pool **867-3080**
Zilker Park

Austin Neighborhood Pools

Admission is free

Call 476-4521 for more information

Balcones .... 12017 Amherst Drive
Brentwood .... 6710 Arroyo Seca
Canyon Vista .... 8455 Spicewood Springs Road
Civitan .... 513 Vargas Road
Dittmar .... 1009 Dittmar Road
Dottie Jordan .... 2803 Loyola Lane
Gillis .... 2501 South First Street

Govalle .... 5200 Bolm Road
Kealing .... 1500 Rosewood Avenue
Kennemer .... 1031 Peyton Gin Road
Martin .... 1601 Haskell Street
Metz .... 2407 Canterbury Street
Montopolis .... 1200 Montopolis
Murchison .... 3700 North Hills Drive

Palm .... 200 North IH-35
Patterson .... 4200 Brookview Road
Ramsey .... 4301 Rosedale Drive
Reed .... 2600 West Pecos Street
Rosewood .... 1182 North Pleasant Valley Road
Shipe .... 4400 Avenue G
St. Edwards .... (on Campus)
St. Johns .... 910 East. St. Johns Avenue
Stacy .... 700 East Live Oak
West Enfield .... 2008 Enfield Road
Zaragoza .... 741 Pedernales Street

Austin Wading Pools

Bailey .... 1101 West 33rd Street
Bartholomew .... 5200 Berkman Drive
Clarksville .... 1811 West 11th Street
East Woods .... 3001 Harris Park Blvd.
Metz .... 2407 Canterbury Street
Odom .... 1010 Turtle Creek Blvd.
Pan American .... 2100 East 3rd Street
Pease .... 1100 Kingsbury Street
Ricky Guerrero .... 500 Brodie Lane

Shipe .... 4400 Avenue G
Stacy .... 2200 Alameda Drive
West Austin .... 1317 West 10th Street

Anderson Mill

Neighborhood Association Pools

Anderson Mill Pool **258-3687**
10701 School House Lane
El Salido Pool **250-8427**
11500 El Salido Pkwy.

CedarPark

City Pools

Buttercup Creek Pool **250-9578**
407 Twin Oak Trail
Elizabeth Milburn Aquatice Facility **331-9317**
1901 Sun Chase Blvd.

Neighborhood Association Pool

Canyon Creek **335-9941**
11321 Boulder Lane

Leander

City Pool

Leanader City Pool **259-8115**
501 South Bagdad

Pflugerville

City Pool

Gilleland Creek Park Pool **251-5082**
700 Railroad Avenue

Round Rock

City Pools

For more information call 218-5540

Lake Creek Municipal Pool ...... 800 Deerfoot Drive
Micki Krebsbach Memorial Pool 301 Deepwood Drive

Brushy Creek

For more information call 255-7871

Cat Hollow Pool .... 8600 O'Connor
Creekside Pool .... 3903 County Road 174

Wells Branch

For more information call 251-9932

Wells Branch .... 2106 Klattenhoff Drive

Area City Parks

Austin

Adams-Hemphill Park .... 201 West 30th Street
Bailey Park .... 1101 West 33rd Street
Balcones District Park .... 12017 Amherst Drive
Bartholomew District Park .... 5201 Berkman Drive
Barton Creek Greenbelt .... 3755 Highway 360
Battlebend Park .... 4600 Suburban Drive
Boggy Creek Greenbelt .... 1114 Nile Street
Brentwood Park .... 6710 Arroyo Seca
Brush Square .... 401 East 5th Street
Bull Creek District Park .... 6701 Lakewood Drive
Buttermilk Branch Greenbelt .... 7500 Meador Avenue
Civitan Park .... 513 Vargas Road

Clarksville Park .... 1811 West 11th Street
Comal Park .... 300 Comal Street
Commons Ford Park .... 614 Commons Ford Road
Dick Nichols Park .... 5011 Beckett Road
Dittmar Park .... 1009 Dittmar Road
Dottie Jordan Park .... 2803 Loyola Lane
Dove Springs Park .... 5801 Ainez Drive
Duncan Park .... 900 West 9th Street
Eastwoods Park .... 3001 Harris Park Avenue
Emma Long Park .... 1600 City Park Road
Franklin Park .... 4800 Copperbend Blvd.
Garrison park .... 6001 Manchaca Road
Gillis Park .... 2501 South First Street
Govalle Park .... 5200 Bolm Road
Gracywoods Park .... 12133 Metric Blvd.
J.J. Seabrook Greenbelt .... 2000 Pershing Drive
Johnson Creek Greenbelt .... 2100 Enfield Road
Joslin Park .... 4500 Manchaca Road
Kealing Park .... 1500 Rosewood Avenue
Kendra Page Park .... 2203 Blue Meadow Drive
Walter E. Long Park .... 6614 Blue Bluff Road
Longview Park .... 7609 Longview Road
Lott Park .... 1108 Curve Street
Mabel Davis Park .... 3427 Parker Road
Martin Park .... 1601 Haskell Street
Mary Moore Searight Park .... 907 Slaughter Lane
Mayfield Park .... 3505 West 35th Street
Montopolis Park .... 1200 Montopolis
Mount Bonnell Park .... 3800 Mount Bonnell Road

North Oaks Park .... 900 Plaza Drive
Northeast District Park ....5909 Crystalbrook Drive
Northwest District Park.................. 7000 Ardath Street
Oak Springs Playground............. 3601 Webberville Road
Oak View Park .... 10800 Oak View Drive
Palm Park .... 200 North IH-35
Parque Zaragoza .... 741 Pedernales Street
Patterson ....4200 Brookview Road
Pease Park .... 1100 Kingsbury Street
Perry Playground.............................. 4900 Fairview Drive
Quail Creek park .... 1101 Mearns Meadow Drive
Ramsey Park ....4301 Rosedale Drive
Red Bud Isle.. 3401 Red Bud Trail
Reed Park .... 2600 West Pecos Street
Republic Square Park .... 422 Guadalupe Street
Ricky Guerrero Park.................... 2006 South 6th Street
Ron Rigsby Park .... 1110 Little Elm
Rosewood Park .... 1182 North Pleasant Valley Road
Shipe Park.. 4400 Avenue G
Slaughter Creek Park ....507 West Slaughter lane
Springfield Park .... 6300 East William Canon
St. Elmo Playground ....4410 South 1st Street
Stacy Park ....700 East Live Oak
T.A. Brown Playground .... 505 West Anderson Lane
Tarrytown Park ....2106 Tower Drive
Walnut Creek Park .... 12138 North Lamar
Walsh Boat Landing ....1600 Scenic Drive
Waterloo Park .... 403 East 15th Street
West Austin Park.......................... 1317 West 10th Street

West Enfield Park .... 2008 Enfield Road
Williams Playground .... 400 Blue Valley Drive
Wooldridge Square .... 900 Guadalupe Street
Wooten Park .... 1406 Dale Drive
Zilker park .... 2220 Barton Springs Road

Cedar Park

Buttercup Creek Park .... Buttercup Creek Blvd.
Cluck Creek .... 901 Rambling Trail
Creekside Park .... Buttercup Creek Blvd.
Cypress Bend Park .... 1604 Iris Lane
Cypress Mill .... 2603 Gold Finch Drive
Elizabeth M. Milburn Park .... 1901 Sun Chase Blvd.
Nelson Ranch Park .... 905 Nelson Ranch Road
New Hope .... 1400 West New Hope
Peggy Garner Park .... Peachtree Drive
Park Place Park .... 101 Vale Drive
Wildrose .... 700 Wildrose Trail

Leander

Leander Park .... Bagdad Road

Pflugerville

Bohls Park .... Dessau Road
Gilleand Creek Park .... 700 Railroad Avenue
Moose Park .... Settlers Valley Drive
Pfluger Park .... City Park Road

Round Rock

Buck Egger Park .... 900 South Mays
Chisholm Valley Park .... 1201 Tray
Creekmont West Park .... Oakridge Drive
Frontier Park .... 1502 Frontier Trail

G.A. Stark Park .... 1409 Provicent
Greenslopes Park .... 1600 Gattis School Road
Henry S. McNeil Park .... 3701 North IH-35
Kensington Place Park .... 1890 Oxford
Lake Creek Park .... 800 Deerfoot Drive
Mesa Village Park .... 1401 Georgetown
Old Settlers Park .... 3300 Palm Valley Road
Round Rock Park .... IH-35 and 620
Round Rock West Park .... 500 Round Rock West
Sam Bass Park .... East Main Street
Settlement Park .... 1400 David Curry
Somerset Park .... 1600 Somerset
Stella Park .... 803 Nance Drive
Veterans Park .... 200 Pecan
Windy Terrace .... 1401 Gattis School Road

Tennis Centers

Call for information on hours, fees and to reserve a court

Caswell Tennis Center 478-6268
24th Street & Lamar Blvd.
Pharr Tennis Center 477-7773
4201 Brookview Road
South Austin Center 442-1466
1000 Cumberland Drive
Town lake Tennis Center 322-9604
1715 West Cesar Chavez Street

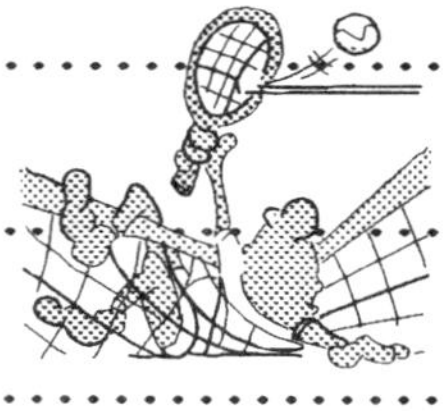

City of Austin Tennis Courts

Call 499-6700 for more information

Austin Recreation Center .... 1301 Shoal Creek Blvd.
Bailey Park .... 1101 West 33rd Street
Bartholomew Park .... 1800 East 51st Street
Brentwood Park .... 6710 Arroyo Seco
Buttermilk Branch Greenbelt .... 7500 Meador Avenue
Civitan Park .... 513 Vargas Road
Dick Nichols Park .... 8011 Beckett Road
Dottie Jordan Park .... 2803 Loyola Lane
East Woods Park .... 3001 Harris Park Avenue
Givens Park .... 3911 East 12th Street
Joslin Park .... 4500 Manchaca Road
Kealing Playground .... 1500 Rosewood
Metz Park .... 2407 Canterbury Street
Northwest Park .... 7000 Ardath

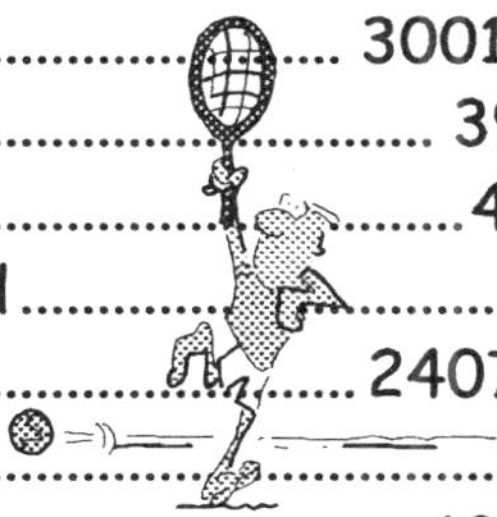

Oakview Park .... 10800 Oak View Drive
Palm Park .... 706 East Cesar Chavez Street
Pan Am Park .... 2100 East 3rd Street
Patterson Park .... 4200 Brookview Road
Perry Park .... 4900 Fairview Drive
Ramsey Park .... 4301 Rosedale Avenue
Rosewood Park .... 1182 North Pleasant Valley Road
Shipe Park .... 4400 Avenue G
Stacy Park .... 1400 Alameda Drive
Wooldridge Park .... 1412 Norseman Terrace
West Enfield Park .... 2008 Enfield Road
Zilker Park .... 1900 Bluebonnet Lane

City of Round Rock Tennis Courts

Admission is free

Call 867-6442 for more information

Frontier Park	1502 Frontier Trail
Greenslopes Park	1600 Gattis School Road
McNeil Park	3701 North IH-35
Round Rock West Park	500 Round Rock West
Stark Place	1409 Provident Lane
Stella Park	803 Nancy Drive

Area School Tennis Courts

These tennis courts are open to the public, unless they are in use by students.

Anderson High School	8403 Mesa Drive
Bowie High School	4103 West Slaughter Lane
Crockett High School	5601 Manchaca Road
LBJ High School	7309 Lazy Creek Drive
Lanier High School	1201 Payton Gin Road
Leander High School	3301 South Bagdad Road
Pflugerville High School	1301 West Pecan Street
Reagan High School	7104 Berkman Drive
Round Rock High School	300 Lake Creek Drive
Travis High School	1211 East Oltorf Street
West Lake High School	4100 Westbank Drive
Westwood High School	12400 Mellow Meadow Drive

City of Austin Municipal Golf Courses

Call for information on hours and fees

Walk-ons welcome

Hancock Golf Course 453-0876
811 East 41st Street

Jimmy Clay Golf Course 444-0999
5400 Jimmy Clay

Lions Municipal Golf Course................. 477-6963
2910 Enfield Road

Morris Williams Golf Course 926-1298
4305 Manor Road

Daily Fee Golf Courses

Bar-K Golf Club 267-1226
Bar-k Ranch Road, Lago Vista

Blackhawk Golf Club 251-9000
225 Kelly Lane, Pflugerville

Bluebonnet Golf Club 272-4228
9100 Decker Lane, Austin

Butler Park Golf Club 477-9025
201 Lee Barton Drive, Austin

Ceders on Bergstrom Golf Club 385-4653
Highway 71, Austin

Circle C Golf Club 288-4297
7401 Highway 45, Austin

Crystal Falls Golf Club 259-5855
3400 Crystal Falls Pkwy., Leander

Forest Creek Golf Club 388-2874
99 Twin Ridge Pkwy., Round Rock

Point Venture Golf Club 267-2768
422 Venture Blvd., Leander

River Place Golf Club 346-6784
4207 River Place Blvd., Austin

Riverside Golf Club 386-7077
1020 Grove Blvd., Austin

Spectator Sports

Professional

Call for tickets and game schedules

Austin Ice Bats 927-7825
Austin Lone Stars 892-7477
Round Rock Express 255-2255

Dallas Cowboys 972/556-9900
Dallas Mavericks 214/748-1808
Dallas Stars 972/868-2890
Houston Astros 713/799-9500
Houston Rockets 713/627-3865
San Antonio Dragons 210/737-2466
San Antonio Missions 210/675-7275
San Antonio Spurs 210/554-7787
Texas Rangers 817/273-5100

College Sports

Call for tickets and game schedules

UT Longhorn's 471-3333
Concordia University 486-1164

Huston-Tillotson University 505-3050
St. Edward's University 448-8480
Southwest Texas State 512/245-2272
Southwestern University 512/863-1381

Recreational Sports

Capital Area Youth Soccer 836-8559
City Softball Leagues 480-3015
Little League Baseball 276-7734
Optimist Club Baseball 453-6852
Volleyball Hotline 467-7148
Texas Mountain Guides 482-9208
Austin Cycling Association 282-1987
Austin Aeronauts 444-3257
Austin Rowing Club 472-0700
Colorado River Walkers 495-6294

Make new friends...........
Join a club

Austin Newcomers Club 314-5100
Austin Country Club
4408 Long Champ Drive
Luncheon at 11:30am the second Thursday of each month
Must be new to the area within the last 2 years.

New Neighbors of Northwest Austin 918-9590
Balcones Country Club, 8600 Balcones Club Drive
Luncheon at 11am the second Wednesday of each month
May remain active indefinitely

Round Rock New Neighbors 388-3796
Damon's, 1801 IH-35 North, Round Rock
Meeting and luncheon the third Wednesday of each month from 10:30am to 1:30pm.
May remain active indefinitely

Austin Area Garden Council 477-8672
Austin Garden Center, 2200 Barton Springs Road

Austin Sierra Club 860-2993
State Conservation Office
1104 Nueces Street

The following groups welcome anyone dedicated to learning, creating and preserving the arts and crafts. Call for meeting times.

Austin Area Quilt Guild 258-5329
Austin Lacemakers 255-2438
Austin Stitchery Guild 328-6528
Austin Woodworkers Club 443-0777
Knitter's & Crocheter's Guild of Texas .. 281-4996

Austin Writer's League 499-8914
1501 West 15th Street, Suite E2
If you love to write check out this group. They offer workshops and informal classes that will help you reach your potential.

Lonestar Group of Mensa 310-9090
Prospective members must score in the top 2% of the population on the standardized IQ test.

Rotary Club of Austin 462-1333
104 Academy Drive

Knights of Columbus 327-1813
2500 Columbus Drive

Lions Club 441-1555
1101 Music Lane

Toastmasters International 479-9280

.... Be a volunteer

Volunteer Center 472-3848
Puts volunteers in contact with non-profit agencies.

Austin Habitat for Humanity 472-8788
310 Comal Street #100
"Austin Habitat for Humanity works in partnership with

God and people everywhere, from all walks of life, to put our faith in action by building affordable quality houses with families in need in order to eliminate poverty housing one house at a time." All construction teams and building crews are volunteers.

The Habitat RE-store **478-2165**
Comal & East 4th Street
Volunteers also run the Re-store, which is a great recycling shop for new and used building materials.

Austin Parks & Recreation **327-6498**
Volunteers help with special programs.

A.I.S.D **499-1701**
Volunteers are needed for the mentor program.

Meals on Wheels **475-6325**
Volunteers prepare and deliver food to the home-bound, disabled and elderly.

Strictly Seniors

Activity Centers

Conley-Guerrero Senior Center **478-7695**
808 Nile Street
Nueces Activity Center **476-5218**
3911 Manchaca Road

Senior Activity Center 474-5921
29th & Lamar

Cedar Park Senior Center 331-6000
408 Ridgewood

Round Rock Senior Center 255-4970
205 East Main

Employment

Austin Senior Aides 480-3006
Offers on the job training with non-profit agencies.

Experience Unlimited 480-3013
Parks and Recreation Department job referral bank for people over age 50.

Old Bakery & Emporium 477-5961
1006 Congress Avenue
Offers people age 50 or older the opportunity to supplement their incomes by selling hand-made and baked goods on consignment.

Foster Grandparents 371-6098
Volunteer opportunity for people 60 and older to spend time with infants and children who need a little love.

When you need help

Texas Department on Aging 444-2727
Offers programs for anyone age 60 and older.

Adult Protective Services 873-6342
Elderly abuse hotline

Family Eldercare Respite Services **467-6168**
In home care for the elderly.
Meals on Wheels **476-6325**
Delivers six meals a week to home bound people.
Groceries to Go **476-6325**
Arranges volunteers to shop for groceries
Handy Wheels **476-6325**
Volunteers help with household repairs

Austin Community Gardens
4814 Sunshine Drive
458-2009

Greenspots Gardens:

Small community gardens for low income individuals, the elderly and people with disabilities.

The Sunshine Rental Garden:

More than 350 gardeners rent plots at the site which uses organic growing methods.

Youth Gardens:

Gardens at elementary and middle schools , enhance the schools' educational efforts, and help promote responsibility and "community building" among students.

Food Bank Garden:

Volunteers plant, maintain and harvest a 7,900 square

foot garden at the Sunshine Garden. It can yield up to 5000 pounds of vegetables per year. The produce is donated to the Capital Area Food Bank and other food pantries.

Educational Programs:
Community workshops and gardening classes on organic gardening and composting.

Yard Waste Drop-off Site:
Leaves and grass clippings are left at the site by homeowners and landscapers; then composted.

Volunteer Programs:
Austin Community Gardens needs volunteers to help maintain the food bank garden, work in gardens at schools and low income communities.

The Great Outdoors

Hunting and Fishing in Texas

Texas Parks and Wildlife 800/792-1112

Fishing Licenses: For residents of Texas, only those between the ages of 17 and 65 years of age are required to have a fishing license. A fishing license is required however, for all nonresident fishermen.

Fees

Resident, annual	**$13.00**
Resident, temporary 14-day	**$10.00**
Nonresistant, annual	**$30.00**
Nonresident, 5-day	**$20.00**

The first Saturday in June of each year is the annual Free Sportfishing Day and no person is required to have a fishing license or stamps while sportfishing on that day.

Resident Combination Hunting and Fishing ... $25.00
Valid for both hunting and fishing for Texas residents only.

Hunting Licenses: A hunting license is required of any person, regardless of age, who hunts in Texas. Residents under 17 or over 65 years of age do not need a regular hunting license, but must have a $6.00 Special Resident Hunting License.

Fees

Resident General Hunting	**$13.00**
Nonresistant General Hunting	**$250.00**
Nonresident Special Hunting	**$100.00**
Nonresident Spring Turkey	**$100.00**
Nonresident 5-day special	**$35.00**

Note: While hunting, fishing or trapping, persons 17 years of age or older must carry on their person a driver's license or personal identification certificate issued by the Department of Public Safety.

Non residents must carry similar documents issued by the agency in their state or country of residence that is authorized to issue driver's licenses or personal identification certificates.

Boating in Texas

Texas Parks & Wildlife	**389-4634**
Travis County Sheriff	**473-9285**
LCRA	**800/776-5272**

Registration: All motorboats regardless of length and sailboats 14 feet in length or over must be registered and titled, and outboard motors must be titled.

Certificate of Number: When your vessel is in operation your registration certificate must always be on board.

Display of Your Number: The number awarded to your vessel must be painted, decaled or otherwise affixed to both sides of the bow of the boat in such a position as to provide easy identification. The number shall read from left to right, must be in block characters of good proportion not less than 3 inches in height, and must be of a color that contrasts with the background.

Personal Flotation Devices: Every recreational vessel must carry at least one U.S. Coast Guard Approved PFD for each person on board. Children under 13 years of age in motorboats less than 26 feet in length must wear a U.S. Coast Guard approved PFD while underway.All Personal Floatation Devices carried on board must be serviceable, readily accessible, and of appropriate size for the intended wearer.

Navigation Lights: Recreational boats must display their required navigation lights at all times between sunset to sunrise, and during daylight periods of reduced visibility.

Anchor Lights: A vessel when not at dock must have and exhibit at least one bright light, lantern, or flashlight from sunset to sunrise in all weather.

Sound Device: All vessels 16 to 26 feet in length must carry a hand, mouth, or power operated whistle on board. All vessels over 26 feet in length must carry a bell.

Watercraft Operation by Teens: Texas law states that all persons between the ages of 13 and 15 must pass a state certified boater education class before they can operate a motorboat with more than 15 hp, a personal watercraft with more than 10 hp or a windblown vessel more than 14 feet in length.
For class information call 389-4999

Personal Watercraft: This includes jet skis and wet bikes. A Coast Guard approved PFD must be worn by each person on or being towed by personal watercraft.

A cutoff or kill switch must be attached to operator or operator's clothing if the vessel is equipped with this device.

The law prohibits any person form operating personal watercraft at night (between sunset and sunrise) or within 50 feet of another vessel, platform, person, object or shore.

Water Skiing: In Texas, water skiing is prohibited from one-half hour after sunset until one-half hour before sunrise. The tow vessel must have an observer 13 years or older or be equipped with a wide angel rear view mirror.

State Parks Around Austin

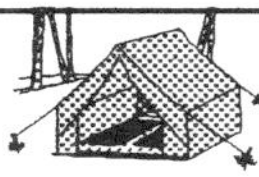

▒ facilities provided

■ facilities permitted but not provided

Park	Daily Entrance Fee	Restrooms	Showers	Camping	RV Sites	Cabins	Screened Shelters	Trailer Dump Station	Group Facility	Trails	Picnics	Swimming	Fishing
Bastrop .... **321-2101** Bastrop	▒	▒	▒	▒	▒	▒			▒	▒	▒	▒	■
Blanco .... **210/833-433** Blanco	▒	▒	▒	▒	▒		▒				▒	■	■
Buescher .... **237-2241** Smithville	▒	▒	▒	▒	▒		▒		▒		▒		
Enchanted Rock ... **210/321-2101** Fredericksburg	▒	▒	▒	▒						▒	▒		
Guadalupe River .... **210/438-2656** Boerne	▒	▒	▒	▒	▒			▒		▒	▒	■	■
Hill Country .... **796-4413** Bandera	▒			■									
Inks Lake .... **512/793-2223** Burnet	▒	▒	▒	▒	▒		▒	▒		▒	▒	■	▒
Kerrville-Schreiner **210/257-5392** Kerrville	▒	▒	▒	▒	▒		▒	▒	▒	▒	▒	■	■
Lockhart .... **398-3479** Lockhart	▒	▒	▒	▒	▒				▒		▒	▒	
McKinney Falls .... **243-1643** Austin	▒	▒	▒	▒	▒		▒	▒	▒	▒	▒	▒	■
Palmetto .... **672-3266** Luling	▒	▒	▒	▒	▒				▒		▒	▒	■
Pedernales Falls .... **868-7304** Johnson City	▒	▒	▒	▒	▒				▒		▒	▒	■

Fees at all parks vary

Children age 12 and under free

The Highland Lakes

There are seven lakes in the Highland Lakes chain, which were formed by dams on the Colorado River. They run through 150 miles of the Hill Country.

Lake Name

Park Name - Operated By

▒ facilities provided

■ facilities permitted but not provided

* reservations only

Lake Name / Park Name - Operated By	Daily Entrance Fee	Annual Permit Avail	Day Use Only	Restrooms	Showers	Camping	RV Sites	Trailer Dump	Station	Group Facility	Trails	Picnic	Boat Ramp
Buchanan 23,060 acres													
Black Rock - LCRA	▒			▒		▒		▒			▒		▒
Buchanan Dam - Burnet County						■						▒	▒
White Bluff - Burnet County				▒		▒					▒	▒	▒
Cedar Point Primitive Area - LCRA									▒		▒	▒	
Llano County - Llano County						▒					▒	▒	▒
Inks 803 acres													
Inks Lake State Park - Texas Parks & Wildlife	▒		▒	▒	▒	▒	▒	▒	▒	▒	▒	▒	▒
LBJ 6,375 acres													
Cottonwood Primitive Area - LCRA			▒									▒	▒
*Kingsland Archaeological Site-LCRA			▒	▒						▒	▒		
Kingsland - Lions Club			▒									▒	▒
Marble Falls 780 acres													
Lakeside - City of Marble Falls			▒	▒							▒	▒	▒
Falls Creek - City of Marble Falls			▒	▒							▒		
Johnson - City of Marble Falls				▒		▒					▒	▒	▒
Travis 18,930 acres													
Arkansas Bend - Travis County	▒	▒		▒		▒					▒	▒	▒
Camp Creek - LCRA						■				▒	▒	▒	▒
*Chautauqua-Adopt Colorado Found	▒			▒	▒	▒	▒	▒	▒	▒	▒	▒	▒
Cypress Creek - Travis County	▒	▒		▒		▒					▒	▒	▒
Gloster Bend Primitive Area - LCRA						■							▒

Lake Name
Park Name - Operated By

▒ facilities provided
█ facilities permitted but not provided
* reservations only

Lake Name / Park Name - Operated By	Daily Entrance Fee	Annual Permit Avail	Day Use Only	Restrooms	Showers	Camping	RV Sites	Trailer Dump Station	Group Facility	Trails	Picnic	Boat Ramp
Travis - continued												
Grelle Primitive Area - LCRA	▒	▒									▒	
Tom Hughes -Travis County	▒	▒									▒	
Mansfield Dam - Travis County				▒		▒		▒			▒	▒
Muleshoe Bend Primitive Area-LCRA								▒			▒	
Narrows Primitive Area - LCRA										▒	▒	
Pace Bend - Travis County	▒	▒		▒		▒	▒	▒		▒	▒	▒
Dink Pearson - Travis County				▒		▒					▒	▒
Sandy Creek - Travis County	▒	▒		▒		▒		▒			▒	▒
Shaffer Bend Primitive Area - LCRA											█	
Turkey Bend East Primitive - LCRA										▒	█	
Bob Wentz at Windy Point - LCRA	▒	▒		▒	▒	▒	▒	▒	▒	▒	▒	▒
Austin 1,830												
Commons Ford - City of Austin			▒						▒	▒	▒	
Fritz Hughes - Travis County			▒								▒	
Selma Hughes - Travis County			▒	▒							▒	
Emma Long - City of Austin	▒			▒	▒	▒	▒	▒	▒		▒	▒
Loop 360 Boat Ramp - Travis Co			▒	▒							█	▒
Mary Quinlan - Travis County			▒	▒							▒	▒
Walsh Boat Landing - City of Austin			▒								▒	▒

Burnet County 512/756-4297
City of Marble Falls 210/693-3615
Travis County 512/473-9437
Llano County 915/247-4352
City of Austin 512/499-6700
Lion Club 915/388-4808
Texas Parks & Wildlife . 800/793-2223
Adopt Colorado Fund ... 512/264-1752

Call for a free
park packet with map
LCRA..... 473-4083

Nature Preserves

These preserves are dedicated to the protection and development of native plants and animals. You will find acres of wooded land with streams and caves, meadows and hills to provide a tranqil, natural setting.

Barrow Preserve
7715 Long Point Drive

Bee Creek
3800 Red Bud Trail

Big Walnut Creek
North of Northeast District Park

Blunn Creek
1100 block of St. Edwards Drive

Balcones Canyonlands
8000 North Capital of Texas Hwy.

Colorado River
Northwest corner of South US 183 and Colorado River

Hamilton Pool **264-2740**
Located on RM 3238, 13 miles south of Texas 71 East

Karst
3900 Deer Lane

Mayfield
3801 West 35th Street

Wild Basin Wilderness **327-7622**
Located on Hwy. 360, 1-1/4 miles north of Bee Cave Rd.

Zilker Park Nature Preserve **327-8181**
301 Nature Center Drive

Special Rules: No firearms, hunting, fishing, motorized vehicles, bicycles, food, drink or pets; removal of anything is prohibited; stay on the trails.

Our Environment

Curbside Recycling

Yard Trimmings

The Big Stuff

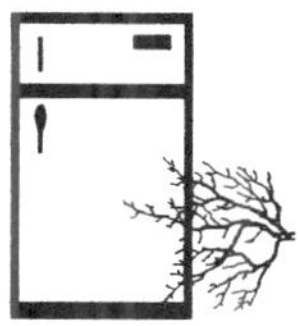

Alternatives to Common Household Products

Watering Tips

'Dillo Dirt

Check with your city for your designated recycling day.

If you are serviced by a private disposal company call to establish recycling service.

Paper Products

Newspaper, including inserts; magazines and shopping catalogues; junk mail and home office paper

- Stack in a paper grocery sack
- Place next to your recycling container
- Currently you cannot recycle pressboard (cereal boxes, beverage containers)

Metal, Plastic and Glass

Aluminum and tin/steel food cans, glass bottles and jars, plastic milk jugs and plastic soda bottles

- Remove food residue and lids
- Labels are OK
- No window glass, Pyrex or dishes
- Flatten plastic
- Place all together in the recycling container

Corrugated cardboard

- Please do not include cereal boxes, shoe boxes, beverage cartons, or pizza boxes.
- Flatten boxes to less than 2-1/2 feet on any side
- Extra brown paper grocery bags can be bagged separately or bundled with corrugated cardboard

The City of Austin also....... Recycles yard waste

The City of Austin composts yard trimmings into '**Dillo Dirt**' a natural fertilizer used in landscaping City parks or sold to the public through local nurseries.

Grass clippings, leaves and twigs

- Place in biodegradable kraft paper bags available at local stores or other reusable container
- Do not use plastic bags

Branches

- No bigger than 5 feet long and 3 inches in diameter
- Tie branches with string (not wire) in bundles

Recycles bulky items

This service is provided twice a year and you will be notified in advance of your scheduled collection week.

Items which CAN be picked up: doors, furniture, appliances, passenger car tires removed from rims, lawn mowers, railroad ties, pallets, rolled fencing and lumber that is nail free.

Brush and tree limbs: stack loosely in piles no higher than 3-1/2 feet with cut ends facing the street. Do not tie or bind in any way. Brush should be 5 to 15 feet long and no thicker than 8 inches in diameter.

Items which <u>CANNOT</u> be picked up: hazardous materials, automotive bodies, motorcycles, trailers and boats; construction and remodeling debris including plywood, bricks, rocks, cinder blocks, stone, concrete, mortar, sand, sheet rock, insulation, flooring, shingles, siding, steel roofing, sheet glass and mirrors.

Need an incentive to recycle? The city of Austin has a pay-as-you throw program. The amount you pay for garbage collection is based on the size of your trash container, 30, 60 or 90 gallons. If you have extra trash you must place it in a plastic bag and use a garbage sticker. The stickers cost $2.00 each and are available at grocery and convenience stores.

Round Rock Recycling

Round Rock Recycling Center **218-7047**
301 Deepwood Drive
Hours: 9:30 am-5:00 pm, seven days a week
No glass containers are accepted at this time.

Private Disposal Companies

Browning Ferris Industries **247-5647**
Longhorn Community Disposal **272-4341**
M & M Disposal **892-1200**
Mid-Tex Waste System **282-3508**
On The Road Salvage **389-1119**
Patterson Disposal **836-3466**

Disposal of Miscellaneous Items

What to do with garage sale leftovers and stuff you can't even give away. Call for times, prices and guidelines.

Austin Community Landfill **272-4329**
9900 Giles Road

BFI Landfill **272-4327**
9912 Giles Road

City of Austin FM 812 Landfill **243-1200**
10108 FM 812

Williamson County Landfill **759-8881**
600 County Road 128

BFI Recycling **385-7600**
4712 Bolm Road, Austin

Commercial Metals **442-2384**
710 Industrial Blvd., Austin

Habitat for Humanity Restore **478-2165**
310 Comal Street

Motor Oil and Antifreeze

Most auto repair shops and service stations will accept used motor oil and antifreeze.

Hazardous Materials

Hazardous Home Chemical Collection Facility
4411 Meinardus Drive **416-8998**

Hours: Wednesday between noon and 7:00 pm
This facility is for Travis County residents only.

For more information call:

The Environmental hotline 800/CLEANUP

Environmentally-Friendly Alternatives to Common Household Products

Many of the chemicals and cleaners used in and around the home can cause water pollution and are hazardous to fish and wildlife. Please consider nontoxic or less-toxic alternatives.

Cleaners

Clogged Drain Openers: Pour one cup baking soda down drain followed by one cup vinegar. Cover the drain tightly for one minute then flush with boiling water.

General Cleanser: Stir 1/2 cup of borax into one gallon of water.

Air Fresheners: Place open containers of baking soda around the house as a deodorizer.

Furniture Polish: Use a mixture of two parts olive oil or vegetable oil with one part lemon juice.

Glass: Mix two teaspoons white vinegar in one cup of warm water.

Oven: Warm the oven, moisten any spills, sprinkle them with baking soda or salt and scrub.

Floor: Mix half cup vinegar to one gallon water.

Scrubbing Powder: Use baking soda or borax.

Household Pesticides

Ant Repellent: Sprinkle chili powder around possible entry areas. Wash kitchen counter with equal parts vinegar and water. Plant pennyroyal, peppermint and tansy plants around your home.

Roach Powder: Dust a very thin film of boric acid powder or Drione on surfaces and into cracks and crevices. Boric acid is also an effective way to control ants. Keep boric acid out of reach of children and pets and do not place on food preparation surfaces.

Moth Repellents: Use cedar chips or lavender flowers in storage areas.

Flea and Tick Control: Vacuum carpets every day for a week and throw away the vacuum bag each day. Treat carpets and floors with products containing insect growth regulators. Shampoo your dog with an insecticidal soap; use a flea comb to remove surviving fleas. Sprinkle brewer's yeast or garlic on your pet's food to deter fleas. Place eucalyptus leaves in your pet's sleeping area.

Lawn Pesticides and Chemicals

Control Mosquitoes: Eliminate sources of standing water and plant mint in your yard. Use larvacides like pyrethume "tossits."

Control Fire Ants: Use less toxic products like Acsend, Logic or Amdro. Be sure to apply according to instructions on the label.

Control Aphids and Spider Mites: Mix a few drops of liquid dishwasher soap in a quart of water and spray the mixture on plants (spraying every three days for a nine-day period interrupts their egg cycle).

Control Fleas: Apply insecticidal soaps or products containing pyrethrins to the infested areas. Although these are preferable to many other products, they are toxic to fish and wildlife if they run off into storm sewers and waterways. To significantly deter fleas, treat your house, your yard and your pet at the same time.

Plant Natural Insect Repellents: Marigolds, mint, pennyroyal, basil, tansy, sage, rosemary and garlic will help discourage pests in your lawn and garden.

Use Biological Controls to Repel Insects: Use bacillus thuringiensis (Bt) for caterpillar control or ladybugs and green lacewings to control a variety of pests. These are available at most organic gardening centers.

Paint Products

Use water based, paints, natural earth pigment finishes and water based wood preservatives; use sandpaper or a heat gun instead of a liquid furniture stripper.

Plant Natural Insect Repellents: Marigolds, mint, pennyroyal, basil, tansy, sage, rosemary and garlic will help discourage pests in your lawn and garden.

SIMPLE STEPS TO PLANTING A TREE

When to plant. Trees grown in containers can be planted at any time. October through March is the best in Austin. This will allow the roots of your new tree to become established before our hot dry summer.

Select the right tree for the right place. Proper tree planting begins with good planning. Determine your planting goals and match the mature size, soil and moisture requirements to the site.

Mark out a planting area 2 to 5 times wider than the root ball diameter (the wider the better). Loosen this area to about an 8" depth. This will enable your tree to extend a dense mat of tiny roots well out into the soil in the first one to ten weeks in the ground.

In the center of the planting area dig a hole at least twice as wide as the root ball and no deeper than the depth of the soil in the root ball. The bottom of the root ball should rest on solid undisturbed soil. When finished, you want the soil at the base of the tree to be at the same level on the tree as it was in the container. The roots also need to get the same ratio of air to water that they received when the tree was in the container or at its original site. Resting the tree on solid ground prevents excessive settling.

Make sure the sides of the hole are rough and uneven. In very hard soils, a rough edge to the hole may help force new roots to grow out into the surrounding soil.

Place the tree in the hole. If the tree is in a container, pull the container away from the root ball. Don't pull the tree out by its trunk. Pulling the tree out of the container by its trunk can damage the small roots within the ball. Place the root ball in the center of the hole and adjust the tree so it is straight and at the proper level. Stand back and look at the tree now, before you put the soil back into the hole. You can make fine adjustments at this time without seriously harming the root ball.

For balled and burlapped trees, rest the root ball in the center of the hole, and reshape the hole so the tree will be straight. After adjusting the tree, pull the burlap and any other material away from the sides and top of the root ball. Don't try to get the material out of the hole, just let it rest beneath the root ball of the tree. Exposing the sides of the root ball to the soil will enable the tree's roots to grow in the most important directions. If you adjust or lift the tree after it's ball has been unwrapped, chances are that the root will be damaged.

Backfill with the original soil. Do not add fertilizer, compost or other material with the original soil. If the backfill soil around the root ball is improved, the tree may be slow in developing a good widespread root system.

Fill until the hole is half full. Flood the hole with a slow hose or tamp gently with your foot to firm the soil.

Repeat until the hole is full. Do not press too firmly, only firmly enough to hold the tree upright. The best soil for root growth has spaces for both air and water; however, large air pockets can cause problems. This method of backfilling with soil and water or gently tamping will remove these large pockets.

Construct a small dam or berm three feet in diameter around the tree. This will help hold water until it soaks into the soil, rather than letting it run off across the surface.

Cover the entire loosened area of soil with 3 to 4 inches of mulch, compost or dry leaves. Mulch will slow water loss, reduce competition from weeds and grasses, will moderate soil temperature and will provide a small amount of nutrients. Keep the mulch away from the base of the trunk to avoid potential rotting of the bark.

It is not necessary to prune a tree at the time of planting unless it is to remove dead, diseased or damaged branches, crossed or rubbing branches, narrow crotches, or multiple main stems

Ten Outdoor Watering Tips

Water your lawn only when it's thirsty: To test whether your lawn needs soaking: step on the grass, if it springs back up, you do not need to water; if it stays flat, it's time to water again. A general rule is to water every five to six days in hot weather.

Water your lawn deeply:
A good soaking encourages deep, solid root growth. Deep rooted lawns are more drought tolerant and winter hardy. A frequent, light sprinkling is the least effective method of watering and can be harmful to your lawn.

Water in the early morning or evening:
Do not water between the hours of 11:00 am and 6:00 pm because water evaporates during the hottest part of the day. Also when hot sunlight hits water droplets on leaves, scalding or burn damage can occur.

Use an effective sprinkler:
For the least amount of evaporation and wind interference, use sprinklers that send water close to the ground rather than high in the air. Big drops are better than fine mists.

Raise mowing height to reduce water needs:
Grass mowed to 2 to 3 inches maintains a deeper root system than grass mowed at 1 inch. Deeper roots need less supplemental water. Mow St. Augustine, blue grass and tall fescue at 3 inches in dry weather. Do not mow Bermuda grass and Zoysia higher than 2 inches.

Use a soaker hose:
Water is often wasted when individuals attempt to water the far corners of the lawn, and the strip of grass between the sidewalk and the street.

Water trees and shrubs separately:
Trees and shrubs, especially those that are newly planted, need a deeper watering than a sprinkler system can provide. Soaker hoses and drip irrigation are efficient watering devices to place around a tree or a bed of shrubs. Allow a soaker hose or drip irrigation system to run lightly for several hours at a time. During the heat of the summer, trees and shrubs can be watered as infrequently as every other week, as long as they are watered deeply. Grass should be kept away from the base of trees and shrubs to allow for greater moisture penetration to the root zone. A 2 to 3 inch layer of mulch at the base of the tree or shrub will also keep the soil cool and improve moisture retention.

Prevent thatch build-up: Thatch is the organic layer between the soil and the green leaves, which can slow water movement into the soil and cause excess runoff. Thatch accumulation results from heavy fertilization, improper mowing, over watering and frequent pesticide use. Aeration and thatch removal increase water penetration and reduce runoff and evaporation. Core aerifiers may be rented at your local equipment center. Under some conditions, wetting agents (surfactants) improve water absorption in a heavily thatched lawn.

Avoid high nitrogen fertilizers in the summer: Heavy application rates of soluble nitrogen fertilizers should be avoided in the summer months. Adding this type of fertilizer to your lawn is like adding salt. Salt causes your lawn to be more thirsty, and require more water. Spring and fall fertilizer applications meet most grass requirements for nutrients without significantly increasing water needs. When lawns appear yellow due to iron deficiency, apply iron sulfate to improve color without increasing water needs. If soils already contain high amounts of sodium salts, adding gypsum improves water absorption.

Install a drought tolerant grass:
Drought tolerance of common turfgrasses:
Excellent --- Buffalograss
Good ---- Common Bermuda and Zoysia
Fair --- St. Augustine and "Tif" Bermuda
Poor ---Tall Fescue, Kentucky
Bluegrass, Ryegrass

The Edwards Aquifer

The Edwards Aquifer, located in the south central part of Texas, is made up of thick layers of porus, honeycombed limestone rock formations.

The aquifer is divided into three distinct regions:

Southern Edwards segment begins at Bracketville in Kinney County and extends through Uvalde, Hondo, San Antonio, New Braunfels and San Marcos.

Barton Springs segment begins near Kyle and extends north through Austin to the Colorado River.

Northern Edwards segment extends from the Colorado River through Georgetown into Bell County near Salado.

Each segment has a contribution zone where watersheds of creeks and rivers catch rainfall and provide the majority of water available for recharge. The major contribution streams for the Barton Springs segment are Onion, Little Bear, Bear, Slaughter, Williamson and Barton.

Barton Springs provides a portion of Austin's drinking water after its flow enters Town Lake and then the City's Green Water Treatment Plant.

The Edwards Aquifer is a fragile resource whose water is threatened by every potential source of pollution that can make its way into the aquifer's intricate structure. Protection, conservation and enhancement are important to those who drink its water and to others who utilize this resource.

Back To School

School Registration

Call the school your child will attend for the times and dates of registration and orientation.

Elementary: Parents must register children who are new to the school district or who transfer to another school . All students entering the school district for the first time must bring a certified immunization record. Students changing schools should bring their report card.

Middle School: Students new to the district and those not already registered with a specific school need to register. All students entering the school district for the first time must bring a certified immunization record. Students changing schools should bring their report card.

High School: Students should have their previously attended school mail a transcript of work completed to the high school they will attend. Students entering the school district for the first time must bring a certified immunization record.

Immunizations

Diptheria\Pertussis\Tetanus

Four doses are required for children age 6 or younger, with one dose on or after the 4th birthday. 3 doses are required for children age 7 or older, with one dose on or after the 4th birthday; Tetanus\Diptheria booster every 10 years after age 5.

Polio

Three doses are required; the last dose must be received the month before, during the month, or after the month of age 4; not required for students 18 years of age or older.

Measles

Two doses are required; one dose on or after the first birthday; Children born on or after September 2, 1991 need to have the second dose before entering school. Children born before September 2, 1991, need to have the second dose before they turn 12.

Rubella: 1 dose required on or after the first birthday.

Mumps: 1 dose required on or after the first birthday.

TB skin test with reading: One TB skin test with reading, within the child's lifetime is required.

HIB CV: 1 dose 15 months through 5 years.

School Bus Eligibility

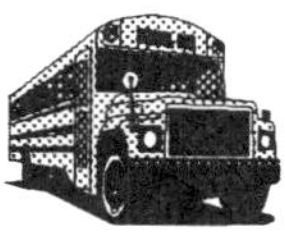

A student must live more than two miles from the assigned school.
Transfer students are not eligible to ride a school bus.

Community Schools

The Austin ISD and Round Rock ISD make full use of their campuses by holding informal classes during their off-hours. For children, this program includes an after school care program, tutoring, arts, sports and summer camps. Adults are offered a variety of courses too, from languages to computers to country western dancing.

Austin ISD Main Campuses

Becker Community School **414-2019**
906 West Milton 78704

Bedichek Community School **414-8919**
6800 Bill Hughes Road 78745

Murchison Community School **346-8930**
3700 North Hills Drive 78731

Webb Community School **450-0914**
601 East St. Johns Avenue 78752

Round Rock ISD Campuses

Round Rock Community School **255-3450**
300 Lake Creek Drive 78681

Westwood Community School **258-8224**
12400 Mellow Meadow Lane 78750

Area School Districts

Austin ISD........414-1700
1111 West 6th Street 78703

Austin High Schools

Anderson High School.......................414-2538
8403 Mesa Drive 78759

Austin High School.........................414-2505
1715 West Cesar Chavez 78703

Bowie High School..........................414-5247
4103 Slaughter Lane 78749

Crockett High School.......................414-2532
5601 Manchaca Road 78745

Johnston High School.......................414-5810
1012 Arthur Stiles Road 78721

Lanier High School.........................414-2514
1201 Payton Gin Road 78758

LBJ High School............................414-2543
7309 Lazy Creek Drive 78724

McCallum High School.......................414-2519
5600 Sunshine Drive 78756

Reagan High School.........................414-2523
7104 Berkman Drive 78752

Travis High School.........................414-2527
1211 East Oltorf 78704

Austin Middle Schools

Bailey Middle School **414-5432**
4020 Lost Oasis Hollow 78739
Bedichek Middle School **414-3265**
6800 Bill Hughes Road 78745
Burnet Middle School **414-3225**
8401 Hathaway 78758
Covington Middle School **414-3276**
3700 Convict Hill Road 78749
Dobie Middle School **414-3270**
1200 East Rundberg Lane 78753
Fulmore Middle School **414-3207**
201 East Mary Street 78704
Kealing Middle School **414-3214**
1701 Pennsylvania Avenue 78702
Lamar Middle School **414-3217**
6201 Wynona 78757
Martin Middle School **414-3243**
1601 Haskell 78702
Mendez Middle School **414-3284**
5106 Village Square 78744
Murchison Middle School **414-3254**
3700 North Hills Drive 78731
O Henry Middle School **414-3229**
2610 West 10th Street 78703
Pearce Middle School **414-3234**
6401 North Hampton 78723
Porter Middle School **414-3236**
2206 Prather Lane 78704
Webb Middle School **414-3258**
601 East St. Johns Avenue 78752

Austin Elementary Schools

Allan Elementary **414-2304**
4900 Gonzales 78702

Allison Elementary **414-2604**
515 Vargas Road 78741

Andrews Elementary **414-1770**
6801 Northeast Drive 78723

Barrington Elementary **414-2008**
400 Cooper Drive 78753

Barton Hills Elementary **414-2013**
2108 Barton Hills Drive 78704

Becker Elementary **414-2019**
906 West Milton 78704

Blackshear Elementary **414-2021**
1712 East 11th Street 78702

Blanton Elementary **414-2026**
5408 Westminister Drive 78723

Boone Elementary **414-2537**
8101 Croftwood Drive 78749

Brentwood Elementary **414-2039**
6700 Arroyo Seca 78757

Brooke Elementary **414-2043**
3100 East 4th Street 78702

Brown Elementary **414-2047**
505 West Anderson Lane 78752

Bryker Woods Elementary **414-2054**
3309 Kerby Lane 78703

Campbell Elementary **414-2056**
2613 Rogers Avenue 78722

Casis Elementary **414-2062**
2710 Exposition Blvd. 78703

Cook Elementary **414-2510**
1511 Cripple Creek 78758

Cunningham Elementary **442-4627**
2200 Berkley Avenue 78745

Davis Elementary **414-2580**
5214 Duval Road 78727

Dawson Elementary **414-2070**
3001 South 1st Street 78704

Doss Elementary **414-2365**
7005 Northledge 78731

Galindo Elementary **414-1756**
3800 South 2nd Street 78704

Govalle Elementary **414-2078**
3601 Govalle Avenue 78702

Graham Elementary **414-2395**
11211 Tom Adams Drive 78753

Gullett Elementary **414-2082**
6310 Treadwell Blvd. 78731

Harris Elementary **414-2085**
1711 Wheless Lane 78723

Highland Park Elementary **414-2090**
4900 Fairview 78731

Hill Elementary **414-2369**
8601 Tallwood Drive 78759

Houston Elementary **414-2517**
5409 Ponciana Drive 78744

Jordan Elementary **414-2538**
6711 Johnny Morris Road 78724

Joslin Elementary **414-2094**
4500 Manchaca Road 78745

Kiker Elementary **414-2584**
913 LaCrosse Avenue 78748

Kocurek Elementary **414-2547**
9800 Curlew Drive 78748

Langford Elementary **414-1765**
2206 Blue Meadow 78744

Lee Elementary **414-2098**
3308 Hampton Road 78705

Linder Elementary **414-2398**
2800 Metcalfe Road 78741

Maplewood Elementary **414-4402**
3808 Maplewood Avenue 78722

Mathews Elementary **414-4406**
906 West Lynn 78703

Menchaca Elementary **414-2333**
12120 Manchaca Road 78748

Metz Elementary **414-4408**
2101 Willow Street 78702

Norman Elementary **414-2347**
4101 Tannehill Lane 78721

Oak Hill Elementary **414-2336**
6101 Patton Ranch Road 78735

Oak Springs Elementary **414-4413**
3601 Webberville Road 78702

Odom Elementary **444-2388**
1010 Turtle Creek Blvd. 78745

Ortega Elementary **414-4417**
1135 Garland Avenue 78721

Palm Elementary **414-2545**
7601 Dixie Drive 78744

Patton Elementary **414-1780**
6001 Westcreek Drive 78749

Pease Elementary **414-4428**
1106 Rio Grande 78701

Pecan Springs Elementary **414-4445**
3100 Rogge Lane 78723

Pillow Elementary **414-2350**
3025 Crosscreek Drive 78757

Pleasant Hill Elementary **414-4453**
6405 Circle S Road 78745

Reilly Elementary **414-4464**
405 Denson Drive 78752

Ridgetop Elementary **414-4469**
5005 Caswell Avenue 78751

Sanchez Elementary **414-4423**
73 San Marcos Street 78702

Sims Elementary **414-4402**
1203 Springdale Road 78721

St. Elmo Elementary **442-3636**
600 West St. Elmo Road 78745

Summitt Elementary **414-4484**
12207 Brigadoon 78727

Sunset Valley Elementary **414-2392**
3000 Jones Road 78745

Travis Heights Elementary **414-4495**
2010 Alameda Drive 78704

Walnut Creek Elementary **414-4499**
401 West Braker Lane 78753

Widen Elementary **414-2556**
5606 Nuckols Crossing 78744

Williams Elementary **414-2525**
500 Mairo 78748
Winn Elementary **414-2390**
3500 Susquehanna Lane 78723
Wooldridge Elementary **414-2353**
1412 Norseman Terrace 78757
Wooten Elementary **414-2315**
1406 Dale 78758
Zavala Elementary **414-2318**
310 Robert Martinez, Jr. Street 78702
Zilker Elementary **414-232**
1900 Bluebonnet Lane 78704

Eanes ISD 329-3600
601 Camp Craft Road 78746

High School

Westlake High School **432-0041**
4100 Westbank Drive 78746

Middle Schools

Hill Country Middle School **327-3771**
1300 Walsh Tarleton 78746
West Ridge Middle School **263-3144**
9201 Scenic Bluff Drive 78746

Elementary Schools

Barton Creek Elementary **263-3518**
1370 Patterson Road 78746
Bridge Point Elementary **347-1881**
6401 Cedar Street 78746

Cedar Creek Elementary **327-5510**
3301 Pennacle Road 78746
Eanes Elementary **327-0337**
4101 Bee Caves Road 78746
Forest Trail Elementary **328-1416**
1203 Capitol of Texas Hwy. South 78746
Valley View Elementary **327-7420**
1201 Capitol of Texas Hwy. South 78746

Lago Vista ISD 267-8300
10801 FM 1431 78645

Lago Vista High School **267-8315**
FM 1431 Lago Vista, Texas 78645
Lago Vista Middle School **267-8305**
FM 1431 Lago Vista, Texas 78645
Lago Vista Elementary School **267-8340**
FM 1431 Lago Vista, Texas 78645

Lake Travis ISD 263-4400
3322 RR 620 South 78734

Lake Travis High School **263-4444**
3322 RR 620 South 78734
Lake Travis Middle School **263-4500**
3322 RR 620 South 78734
Lake Travis Elementary School **266-3352**
3322 RR 620 South 78734
Lakeway Elementary School **261-4336**
1701 Lohmans Crossing 78734

Leander ISD 434-5000

401 S. West Street 78641

High School

Leander High School **435-8000**
3801 South Bagdad Road 78641

Middle Schools

Cedar Park Middle School **434-5025**
2100 Sun Chase 78613

Leander Middle School **434-7800**
410 South West Street 78641

Elementary Schools

Block House Creek Elementary **259-5103**
401 Creek Run Drive 78641

Cypress Elementary **331-0266**
2900 El Salido Pkwy. 78613

Faubion Elementary **258-6627**
1209 Cypress Creek Road 78613

Giddens Elementary **434-7050**
300 South West Street 78641

North Mason Elementary **434-5036**
1501 North Lakeline Blvd. 78641

South Mason Elementary **434-5036**
1501 North Lakeline Blvd. 78613

Steiner Ranch Elementary **434-7100**
4001 North Quinlan Park Road 78732

Whitestone Elementary **259-1911**
2000 Crystal Falls Pkwy. 78641

Pflugerville ISD 251-4159

1401 West Pecan Street Pflugerville, TX 78660

High Schools

Connally High School 252-0040
13212 North Lamar Blvd. 78753

Pflugerville High School 251-2238
1301 West Pecan Sreeet 78660

Middle Schools

Park Crest Middle School 251-2396
1500 Pflugerville Loop 78660

Pflugerville Middle School 251-4123
1600 West Settlers Valley 78660

Westview Middle School 837-7795
1805 Scofield Lane 78727

Elementary Schools

Brookhollow Elementary 251-7711
1200 Pflugerville Loop 78660

Dessau Elementary 251-4690
1501 Dessau Ridge Lane 78753

Northwest Elementary 251-1131
14014 Thermal Drive 78728

Parmer Lane Elementary 837-8001
1806 Parmer Lane 78727

Pflugerville Elementary 251-4155
701 Dessau Road 78660

River Oaks Elementary 832-0772
12401 Scofield Farms Drive 78758

Spring Hill Elementary **990-4716**
600 South Heatherwilde Blvd. 78660
Timmerman Elementary **251-4545**
700 West Pecan Street 78660
Windmere Elementary **251-2414**
1100 Picadilly Drive 78681

Round Rock I.S.D. ... 255-4431
1311 Round Rock Avenue 78681

High Schools

McNeil High School **258-3199**
5720 McNeil Road 78729
Round Rock High School **255-2594**
300 Lake Creek Drive 78681
Westwood High School **464-4000**
12400 Mellow Meadow Drive 78750

Middle Schools

Canyon Vista Middle School **331-1666**
8455 Spicewoods Springs Road 78759
Cedar Valley Middle School **255-9516**
8139 Racine Trail 78717
Chisholm Trail Middle School **255-7866**
500 Oak Ridge Drive 78681
C.D. Fulkes Middle School **255-4471**
300 West Anderson Avenue 78664
Deerpark Middle School **335-5196**
8849 Anderson Mill Road 78729

Grisham Middle School 258-6667
10805 School House Lane 78750

Hopewell Middle School 464-6710
1901 Sunrise 78664

Round Rock Elementary Schools

Anderson Mill Elementary 258-5489
10610 Salt Mill Hollow 78750

Berkman Elementary 255-4411
400 West Anderson Avenue 78664

Bluebonnet Elementary 388-4184
1010 Chisholm Valley Trail 78681

Brushy Creek Elementary 258-1088
2800 Stonebridge Drive 78681

Deepwood Elementary 255-5891
705 St. Williams 78681

Double File Trail Elementary 388-4091
2400 Chandler Creek Blvd. 78664

Fern Bluff Elementary 218-8585
17815 Park Valley Drive 78681

Forest North Elementary 258-6451
13414 Broadmeade Avenue, Austin 78729

Gattis Elementary 218-1122
2920 Round Rock Ranch Blvd. 78664

Jollyville Elementary 335-7756
6720 Corpus Christi Drive 78729

Laural Mountain Elementary 258-1373
10111 D K Ranch Road 78759

North Oaks Elementary 258-2282
11104 Oak View Drive 78759

Old Town Elementary **255-9851**
2001 West Old Settlers 78681

Pond Springs Elementary **258-1610**
7825 Elkhorn Mountain Trail 78729

Purple Sage Elementary **258-3209**
11801 Tanglebriar Trail 78750

Robertson Elementary **255-1321**
1415 Bayland 78681

Spicewood Elementary **258-6667**
11601 Olson 78750

Voigt Elementary **255-3684**
1201 Cushing Drive 78664

Wells Branch Elementary **251-0001**
14650 Merriltown Drive 78728

Continuing Education

Austin Community College **483-7542**

UT Informal Classes **471-0270**

Informal classes provide a variety of short courses, workshops, and certificate programs for the entire Austin community. Call for a schedule. Times, cost and location vary depending on the course.

UT Extension **471-2900**

Evening courses with full college credit. No UT admission is required. Courses offered cover a wide variety of interests, including art, writing, computers and liberal arts courses. Grades as well as credits transfer to a UT transcript.

Colleges & Universities

Austin Community College **223-7000**
5930 Middle Fiskville Road, Austin 78752

ACC Cypress Creek Campus **223-2000**
1555 Cypress Creek Road, Cedar Park, Texas

ACC Eastridge Campus **223-5100**
4100 Ed Bluestein Blvd., Austin

ACC Northridge Campus **223-5959**
11928 Stonehollow Drive, Austin

ACC Pinnacle Campus **223-8001**
7748 Highway 290 West, Austin

ACC Rio Grande Campus **223-3000**
1212 Rio Grande, Austin

ACC Riverside Campus **223-6000**
1020 Grove Blvd., Austin

Concordia University **452-7661**
3400 IH-35 Austin, Texas 78705

Huston-Tillotson College **505-3027**
900 Chicon Street Austin, Texas 78702

St. Edward's University **448-8400**
3001 South Congress Avenue, Austin 78704

Southwest Texas State University ..**512/245-2364**
601 University Drive, San Marcos 78666

Southwestern University **800/252-3166**
Southwestern University, Georgetown 78626

The University of Texas **475-7440**
The University of Texas, Austin 78712

Welcome to the Hill Country

AUSTIN TEXAS

LIVE MUSIC CAPITAL OF THE WORLD

CEDAR PARK TEXAS

Oktoberfest

FREDERICKSBURG

FIRST WEEKEND IN OCTOBER

WIMBERLEY

THE STAR OF TEXAS

Have a question about Texas?

We can steer you in the right direction.

1-800-452-9292

8AM-9PM DAILY

Texas Department of Transportation

Round Rock, Texas

TOUR HISTORIC BASTROP

KERRVILLE Wine & Music FESTIVAL

Burnet

Bluebonnet Capital of Texas

Fredericksburg ...An Enduring Heritage™

March

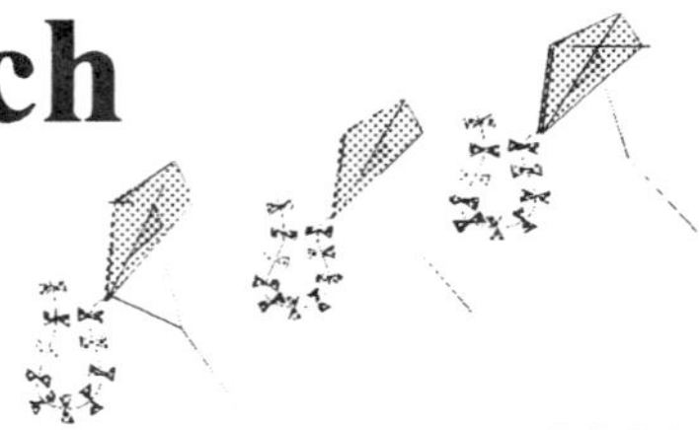

March 12-21
Austin-Travis County
Livestock Show and Rodeo 467-9811
Travis County Exposition Center

March 14
Kite Festival
Zilker Park, Austin

March 17-21
SXSW
Music Festival
467-7979
Various locations, Austin

March 21
Austin Capitol 10K
445-3593
15th Street and Congress Avenue to Auditorium Shores

April

April 9-11
Bluebonnet Arts & Crafts Trail **756-4297**
Burnet, Marble Falls, Llano, Kingsland & Buchanan Dam

April 10
Spamarama **416-9307**
Auditorium Shores, Austin

April 16-17
Old Settlers Music Festival **255-5805**
Old Settlers Park, Round Rock

April 24-25
Safari **327-8181**
Austin Nature Center

April 16-25
Fiesta **800-447-3372**
San Antonio

May

May 1-2
Old Pecan Street Festival **441-9015**
Sixth Street, Austin

May 15-16
Fiesta **458-8191**
Laguna Gloria, Austin

May 8
Cinco de Mayo **250-9400**
Fiesta Gardens, Austin

May 1-2
Mayfair **930-3535**
San Gabriel Park, Georgetown

May 27-June 13
Folk Festival **830/257-3600**
Kerrville

May or June
Cedar Chopper Festival **260-4260**
Cedar Park (Call for exact date)

June

June 11-13
Country Peddler Show 800/775-2774
Fredericksburg

Juneteenth Freedom Festival 459-1181
Austin

June 18-19
Peach Jamboree and Rodeo 830/644-2735
Stonewall

July 3
Willie Nelson 4th of July Picnic 830/997-6523
Fredericksburg

Concert & Fireworks 476-6064
Auditorium Shores, Austin

July 9-11
Spring Ho Festival 512/556-5301
Lampasas

Blues on the Green 338-4437
Courtyard at the Arboretum, Austin

Zilker Summer Musical 479-9491
Zilker Hillside Theatre, Austin

Blanco County Fair **210/868-7684**
Johnson City

August 27-29
Gillespie County Fair **830/997-6523**
Fredericksburg

September

September 3-5
Oatmeal Festival **512/355-2197**
Bertram

September 25-26
Old Pecan Street Festival **478-1704**
East 6th Street, Austin

September 18-October 11
Shakespeare Under the Stars **454-2273**
Zilker Park, Austin

September 18-19
Republic of Texas Chilympiad **512-396-5400**
Hays County Civic Center, San Marcos

October

October 1-3
Frontier Days **255-5805**
Round Rock

October 1-3
Octoberfest **830/997-4810**
Fredericksburg

HALLOWEEN on Sixth Street **478-0098**
Austin

October 31-November 9
Wurstfest **830/625-9167**
New Braunfels

November

November 27-28
Victorian C hristmas **441-9015**
Sixth Street, Austin

November 27, 11:00am.0

Chuy's Blue Santa Parade **888/HEY-CHUY**
The Capitol, south to 6th Street, west to Guadalupe
Donations of unwrapped toys for Blue Santa are appreciated.

November 26-28
Country Peddler Show **800/775-2774**
Fredericksburg

December

December 5
Lighting of the tree in Zilker Park 499-6700

December 13-24, 7pm-10pm
Trail of Lights 499-6700
Zilker Park, Austin

Family Christmas Night 255-5805
Downtown, Round Rock

Area Santa Programs, Blue Santa and Brown Santa, are organized by the area law enforcement departments. To volunteer your time or make donations call your local police or sheriff department.

State Motto: Friendship

State Nickname: Lone Star State

State Flower: Bluebonnet

In late March to early April Bluebonnets blanket the roadsides and meadows.

State Tree: Pecan

Governor James Hogg so loved the pecan tree that his dying wish was to have one planted on his grave and the pecans distributed to the people of Texas for planting.

State Dish: Chili

Chili is the national dish of Texas and every Texan thinks his is the best. This has led to countless chili-cook- offs.

State Bird: Mockingbird

The name comes from their ability to imitate sounds, such as large farm machinery.

State Name: Texas

From the Indian word "tejas" meaning friends.

Six Flags of Texas

Texas Under Spain 1519-1821

Spain was the first European nation to claim Texas lands when in 1519 Cortez arrived in Mexico. It was not until 1681 that Spain established its first settlement in Texas, a mission in present El Paso. Gradually Spain settled the area with other missions and forts and ruled the area until Mexico overthrew the European power and became independent in 1821.

Texas Under France 1685-1690

France's attempt to expand French Louisiana into Texas was short lived. In 1685 La Salle planted a French merchant marine flag in eastern Texas near the Gulf Coast. At this time Spain had no real presence in Texas. By 1690, due to a series of misfortunes, shipwrecks, disease, famine, hostile Indians and internal strife, France had given up on this bold attempt at expansion.

Texas Under Mexico 1821-1836

Mexico encouraged the settlement of Texas by Anglos and Hispanics. They realized it would be easier to hold on to land that was occupied. Early Texas frontiersmen, such as Stephen F. Austin, made land deals with Mexico and brought settlers to the area. When Santa Anna declared himself dictator this escalated the tension, which had developed because of his political attitudes. Texans, Anglo and Hispanic alike demanded and achieved their freedom at the Battle of San Jacinto on April 21, 1836.

Texas as a Republic 1836-1845

Life was not easy for the citizens of the Republic of Texas. Epidemics, financial crises, and clashes with Mexico swayed Texans to join the United States on December 29, 1845. During her 10 years of independence, Texas contributed such legendary figures as the American Cowboys; the Texas Rangers (the first to use Sam Colt's six shooters); and Sam Houston who became the American ideal of rugged individualism.

Texas in the Confederacy 1861-1865

When the American Civil War erupted, Texans chose to join the Confederacy. This choice resulted in devastation and the economic collapse of the state.

Texas as a State 1845-1861; 1865-Present

Through sheer grit and determination, the offspring of the Texas pioneers overcame defeat and reconstruction after the Civil War. Using Texas Longhorns, they were able to provide beef for the nation. The vast acreage yielded crops; while beneath the surface lay its greatest resource of all ...oil. In the early years of the 20th century this discovery led to the making of the legendary Texas millionaires.

Presidents of Texas

David Burnet	1836-1836
Sam Houston	1836-1838
Mirabeau Lamar	1838-1841
Sam Houston	1841-1844
Anson Jones	1844-1845

Governors of Texas

Pickney Henderson	1846-1847
George T. Wood	1847-1849
Peter H. Bell	1849-1853
J.W. Henderson	1853-1853
Elisha Pease	1853-1857
Hardin Runnels	1857-1859
Sam Houston	1859-1861
Edward Clark	1861-1861
Francis Lubbock	1861-1863
Pendleton Murrah	1863-1865
Andrew Hamilton	1865-1866
James Throckmorton	1866-1867
Elisha Pease	1867-1869
Edmund Davis	1869-1874
Richard Coke	1874-1876
Richard Hubbard	1876-1879
Oran Roberts	1879-1883
John Ireland	1883-1887
Lawrence Ross	1887-1891
James Hogg	1891-1895
Charles Culberson	1895-1899
Joseph Sayers	1899-1903
S.W.T. Lanham	1903-1907

Thomas Campbell	1907-1911
Oscar Colquitt	1911-1915
James Ferguson	1915-1917
William Hobby	1917-1921
Pat Morris Neff	1921-1925
Miriam Ferguson	1925-1927
Dan Moody	1927-1931
Ross Sterling	1931-1933
Miriam Ferguson	1933-1935
James Allred	1935-1939
W. Lee O'Daniel	1939-1941
Coke Stevenson	1941-1947
Beuford Jester	1947-1949
Allan Shivers	1949-1957
Price Daniel	1957-1963
John Connally	1963-1969
Preston Smith	1969-1973
Dolph Briscoe	1973-1979
William Clements	1979-1983
Mark White	1983-1987
William Clements	1987-1991
Ann Richards	1991-1995
George W.Bush	1995-

TEXAS was the only state to join the United States and retain its public lands.

TEXAS is the only state that can subdivide if it chooses.

TEXAS was a country before it joined the United States.

The Texas Flag

Star ......Sovereignty
Blue ....Loyalty and friendship
White .....Peace and purity
Red ....Courage and blood shed during war

The white is over the red to symbolize peace over war.
Designer ...Charles B. Stewart ...March, 1836

Johanna Troutman

....The Betsy Ross of Texas

At the age of 18, Johanna Troutman became so inspired by the fight for freedom in Texas that she helped recruit volunteers from Georgia. When they arrived in Texas in 1835, they brought the flag she had designed. The white silk with a five pointed blue star and the legend "Liberty or Death" was one of the earliest flags to represent Texas with a lone star. The flag was destroyed at the battle of Goliad where it had been raised as a symbol of the Texas Republic. Although she never set foot in Texas, Johanna Troutman is buried at the State Cemetery. Her remains were transferred there from Alabama in 1913 by the order of Governor Oscar Colquitt.

Pledge to the Texas Flag

"Honor the Texas Flag.
I pledge allegiance to thee,
Texas, one and indivisible"

The State Song

TEXAS OUR TEXAS

Texas, our Texas! All hail the mighty State!
Texas, our Texas! So wonderful, so great!
Boldest and grandest, withstanding every test
O, empire wide and glorious, you stand supremely blest.

Chorus:
God bless you, Texas! And keep you brave and strong.
That you may grow in power and worth, throughout the ages long.

Refrain:
Texas, O Texas! Your freeborn single star.
Sends out its radiance to nations near and far.
Emblem of freedom! It sets our hearts aglow.
With thoughts of San Jacinto and glorious Alamo.
Texas, dear Texas! From tyrant grip now free.
Shines forth in splendor your star of destiny!
Mother of Heroes! We come your children true.
Proclaiming our allegiance, our faith, our love for you.

The State Seal

The State Seal, made up entirely of Texas stone, was installed in the Capitol during the 1936 Texas Centennial celebration. Originally designed with the letters "Republic of Texas" this was changed in 1845, when Texas became a state. The lone star is wreathed by a live oak branch which symbolizes strength and an olive branch symbolizes peace.

Legend of the Bluebonnet

Texas was ravaged by drought which parched the earth. The Indians were in a struggle for survival as plants and buffalo became scarce. The shaman told his people to offer their most prized possession as a sacrifice. Only one member of the tribe, a little girl, felt she had a gift worthy. Her dearest possession was the doll that had been made by her mother. Her parents and grandparents had died as a result of the drought and this was the only reminder she had of a time when they were with her.

After the others were asleep the child left her tent and went to the open fire and placed her little doll in the flames. The next morning the tribe awoke to find the fields covered in a blanket of flowers as blue as the feather in the dolls hair. As they stood in wonder a gentle rain began to fall.

The Yellow Rose of Texas

Texas won its freedom On April 21, 1836 at the Battle of San Jacinto. This decisive battle lasted only 18 minutes. Part of the success is attributed to a mulatto girl, Emily Morgan. Santa Anna took her from a plantation near Houston to the battlefield. She was able to alert Sam Houston and his men of the Mexican army's plans. Emily kept Santa Anna occupied and Houston was able to take the enemy by surprise. As a reward Emily was granted freedom and immortalized in song.

Pecos Bill

.... A Texas Legend

Legend has it that Pecos Bill was adopted by coyotes after falling from his family's wagon as it headed west. With his horse, Widowmaker, he changed the vast prairie into Texas. While Widowmaker dug the Rio Grande with his hooves, Pecos emptied his boots and made the Davis Mountains, he used his frying pan to scoop out the Palo Duro Canyon and when he wrung out his bandana the Gulf of Mexico was formed.

No one knows for sure what became of this twosome, but some say Widowmaker pitched Pecos higher and higher until he became the brightest star in the Texas sky. The lone star that shines over the great state of Texas.

The Scalping of Joshua Wilbarger

"He says that though paralyzed and unable to move, he knew what was being done, and that when his scalp was torn from his skull it created no pain from which he could flinch, but sounded like distant thunder."

from *Indian Depredations in Texas*
by John Wesley Wilbarger

Joshua Wilbarger and four companions were attacked by Indians while scouting land east of Austin, near Bastrop. Wilbarger survived the arrow wounds and scalping and lived for another 12 years.

Remember the Alamo!

Choosing death over tyranny, the 189 heroes of the Alamo forever found a place in the hearts of all who value freedom. In answer to Travis' plea for reinforcements 32 men and boys from Gonzales made it through the Mexican lines to join the patriots. Some were native Texans of Spanish and Mexican descent who also suffered under the rule of Santa Anna. Others were volunteers, such as Davy Crockett and his Tennessee Boys who owed nothing to Texas, but valued freedom more than life.

Heroes of the Alamo

Juan Abamillo	Texas
R. Allen	unknown
Mills D. Andross	Vermont
Micajah Autry	North Carolina
Juan A. Badillo	Texas
Peter James Bailey	Kentucky
Isaac G. Baker	Arkansas
William C. M. Baker	Missouri
John J. Ballentine	unknown
Robert W. Ballentine	Scotland
John J. Baugh	Virginia
Joseph Bayliss	Tennessee
John Blair	Tennessee
Samuel C. Blair	Tennessee
William Blazeby	England
James Bonham	South Carolina
Daniel Bourne	England
James Bowie	Tennessee
Jesse H, Bowman	unknown
George Brown	England

James Brown	Pennsylvania
Robert Brown	unknown
James Buchanan	Alabama
Samuel E. Burns	Ireland
George D. Butler	Missouri
Robert Campbell	Tennessee
John Cane	Pennsylvania
William R. Carey	Virginia
Charles Henry Clark	Missouri
M.B. Clark	unknown
Daniel W. Cloud	Kentucky
Robert E. Cochran	New Jersey
George W. Cottle	Tennessee
Henry Courtman	Germany
L. Crawford,	South Carolina
David Crockett	Tennessee
R. Crossman,	Massachusetts
David Cummings,	Pennsylvania
Robert Cunningham,	New York
Jacob C. Darst	Kentucky
John Davis	Kentucky
Freeman H.K. Day	unknown
Jerry C. Day	Missouri
Squire Daymon,	Tennessee
William Dearduff	Tennessee
Stephen Dennison	England
Charles Despallier	Lousiana
Almeron Dickinson	Tennessee
John H. Dillard	Tennessee
James R. Dimpkins	England
Lewis Duel	New York
Andrew Duvalt	Ireland
Carlos Espalier	Texas
Gregorio Esparaza	Texas
Robert Evans	Ireland
Samuel B. Evans	New York
James L. Ewing	Tennessee
William Fishbaugh	Alabama
John Flanders	Massachusetts

Dolphin Floyd	North Carolina
John H. Forsyth	New York
Antonio Fuentes	Texas
Gaiba Faqua	Alabama
William H. Furtleroy,	Kentucky
William Garnett	Tennessee
James W. Garrand	Lousiana
James G. Garrett	Tennessee
John E. Gavin	unknown
John E. Gaston	Kentucky
James George	unknown
John C. Goodrich	Tennessee
Albert Calvin Grimes	Georgia
Jose Maria Guerrero	Texas
James C. Gwynne	England
James Hannum	unknown
John Harris	Kentucky
Andrew J. Harrison	unknown
William B. Harrison	Ohio
Charles M. Haskell	Tennessee
Joseph M. Hawkins	Ireland
John M. Hays	Tennessee
Patrick Henry Herndon	Virginia
William D. Hersee	England
Tapley Holland	Ohio
Samuel Holloway	Pennsylvania
William Howell	Massachusetts
William Daniel Jackson	Ireland
Thomas Jackson	Ireland
Green B. Jameson	Kentucky
Gordon C. Jennings	Connecticut
Damacio Jimenes	Texas
Lewis Johnson	Wales
William Johnson	Pennsylvania
John Jones	New York
Johnnie Kellog	unknown
James Kenney	Virginia
Andrew Kent	Kentucky
Joseph Kerr	Louisiana

George C. Kimball	New York
William p. King	unknown
William Irvine Lewis	Virginia
William J. Lightfoot	Virginia
Jonathan I. Lindley	Illinois
William Linn	Massachusetts
Toribio D. Losoya	Texas
George W. Main	Virginia
William T. Malone	Virginia
William Marshall	Tennessee
Albert Martin	Rhode Island
Edward McCafferty	unknown
Jesse McCoy	Tennessee
William McDowell	Pennsylvania
James McGee	Ireland
John McGregor	Scotland
Robert McKinney	Ireland
Eliel Melton,	Georgia
Thomas Miller,	Tennessee
William Mills	Tennessee
Isaac Millsaps,	Mississippi
Edward F. Mitchusson	Virginia
Edwin T. Michell	unknown
Napolean Mitchell	unknown
Robert B. Moore	Virginia
Willis Moore	Virginia
Robert Musselman	Ohio
Andres Nava	Texas
George Neggan,	South Carolina
Andrew M. Nelson	Tennessee
Edward Nelson	South Carolina
George Nelson	South Carolina
James Northcross	Virginia
James Nowlan	Ireland
George Pagan	Mississippi
Christopher Parker	Mississippi
William Parks	North Carolina
Richardson Perry	unknown
Amos Pollard	Massachuettes

John P. Reynolds	Pennsylvania
Thomas H. Roberts	unknown
James Robertson	Tennessee
Issac Robinson	Scotland
James M. Rose	Virginia
Jackson J. Rusk	Ireland
Joseph Rutherford	Kentucky
Manson Shied	Georgia
Issac Ryan	Louisiana
Mial Scurlock	North Carolina
Marcus L. Sewell	England
C. K. Simmons	South Carolina
Andrew H. Smith	Tennessee
Charles S. Smith	Maryland
Joshua G. Smith	North Carolina
William H. Smith	unknown
Richard Starr,	England
James E. Stewart	England
Richard L. Stockton	Virginia
A. Spain Summerlin	Tennessee
William E. Summers,	Tennessee
William D. Sutherland	Alabama
Edward Taylor	Tennessee
George Taylor	Tennessee
James Taylor	Tennessee
William Taylor	Tennessee
B. Archer M. Thomas	Kentucky
Henry Thomas	Germany
Jesse G. Thompson	Arkansas
J. W. Thomson,	North Carolina
John M. Thurston	Pennsylvania
Burke Trammel	Ireland
William B.Travis	South Carolina
George W. Tumlinson	Missouri
James Tylee	New York
Asa Walker	Tennessee
Jacob Walker	Tennessee
William B. Ward	Ireland
Henry Warnell	Arkansas

J. G. Washington	**Tennessee**
Thomas Waters	**England**
William Wells	**Georgia**
Isaac White	**Kentucky**
Robert White	**unknown**
H. Williamson	**Pennnsylvania**
William Wills	**unknown**
David L. Wilson	**Scotland**
John Wilson	**Pennsylvania**
Anthony Wolfe	**England**
C. Wright	**North Carolina**
Charles Zanco	**Denmark**
John, black	**unknown**

William Barret Travis

Commandancy of the Alamo
Bexar Febry. 24, 1836

To the people of Texas & all Americans in the world,

Fellow citizens & compatriots -- I am besieged by a thousand or more of the Mexicans under Santa Anna. I have sustained a continual bombardment and cannonade for 24 hours and have not lost a man. The enemy has demanded a surrender at discretion, otherwise the garrison are to be put to the sword, if the fort is taken. I have answered the demand with a cannon shot and our flag still waves, proudly from the walls. I shall never surrender or retreat. Then, I call on you in the name of Liberty, of patriotism and everything dear to the American character to come to our aid with all dispatch. The enemy is receiving reinforcements daily and will no doubt increase to three or four thousand in four or five days. If this call is neglected, I am determined to sustain myself as long as possible and die like a soldier who never forgets what is due to his honor and that of his country --

VICTORY OR DEATH

William Barret Travis
Lt. Col. Comdt.

James Bowie

Born: May 19,1795 in Tennessee

Jim Bowie was an adventurer who settled in Texas in 1824. He lost his wife and children in a cholera epidemic in 1833. Bowie was the commander of the Alamo until he became ill with pneumonia. Too weak to walk, he valiantly fought his attackers from his cot where he was armed with rifles, and his famous bowie knife.

William Barret Travis

Born: August 1, 1809 in South Carolina

William Travis practiced law before coming to Texas in 1831. He assumed full command of the Alamo when James Bowie became ill. His famous letter written "to all Texans and Americans in the world" is a shining example of the courage and strength of these men. Travis was one of the first to die in the battle with a single shot through his forehead.

David Crockett

Born: August 17, 1786 in Tennessee

Davey Crockett was a frontiersman, soldier and U.S. Congressman. Hearing of the battle for freedom in Texas he arrived at the Alamo in February of 1836 with the Tennessee Mounted Cavalry.

Legend has it that Crockett, out of bullets and wielding his rifle as a club died as thousands of Santa Anna's men stormed the walls. Historians now believe that Davey was captured and executed by Santa Anna after the battle.

Juan Seguin

Born: October 27, 1806 in San Antonio

Although Seguin did not die at the Alamo, he risked his life going through the enemy lines in an attempt to get aid. When he returned to San Antonio to report to Travis that no aid would be coming, the Alamo had fallen. Santa Anna had been so enraged by the battle that he ordered all of the bodies burned. It was Seguin who collected the ashes and saw to their burial.

When Texas became a state its lands stretched farther north and west than today. The U.S. paid Texas 10 million dollars for land that later became parts of New Mexico, Oklahoma, Kansas, Colorado, and Wyoming.

The "Fifty Cent Law of 1879" permitted the sale of unappropriated state lands for 50 cents an acre.

The geographic center is Brady, Texas.

The longest straight line distance north and south is 801 miles; east and west is 773 miles.

Texas consists of 261,914 square miles of land and 5,363 square miles of water

The Austin Handbook

12100 Missel Thrush Court
Austin, Texas 78750
512/219-9476

Need more books?

Please send me ________ copies of **The Austin Handbook.** I have enclosed $14.95 per copy plus $2.50 postage. Texas residents please add $1.23 per book for sales tax.

☐ $18.68 for Texas residents
☐ $17.45 for Non-residents

Name_______________________________________
Address_____________________________________
City______________________State__________Zip________

Make checks payable to The Austin Handbook.

- -

Please send me ________ copies of **The Austin Handbook.** I have enclosed $14.95 per copy plus $2.50 postage. Texas residents please add $1.23 per book for sales tax.

$18.68 for Texas residents
$17.45 for Non-residents

Name_______________________________________
Address_____________________________________
City______________________State__________Zip________

Make checks payable to The Austin Handbook.